SECOND LANGUAGE DEVELOPMENT IN WRITING: MEASURES OF FLUENCY, ACCURACY, & COMPLEXITY

SECOND LANGUAGE DEVELOPMENT IN WRITING: MEASURES OF FLUENCY, ACCURACY, & COMPLEXITY

KATE WOLFE-QUINTERO,
SHUNJI INAGAKI,
& HAE-YOUNG KIM

SECOND LANGUAGE TEACHING & CURRICULUM CENTER
University of Hawai‘i at Mānoa

The contents of this Technical Report were developed under a grant from the Department of Education (CFDA 84.229, P229A60007). However, the contents do not necessarily represent the policy of the Department of Education, and one should not assume endorsement by the Federal Government.

ISBN 0–8248–2069–X

Book design by Deborah Masterson

Distributed by
University of Hawai'i Press
Order Department
2840 Kolowalu Street
Honolulu, HI 96822

ABOUT THE
NATIONAL FOREIGN LANGUAGE RESOURCE CENTER

The Second Language Teaching and Curriculum Center of the University of Hawai'i is a unit of the College of Languages, Linguistics, and Literature. Under a grant from the US Department of Education, the Center has since 1990 served as a National Foreign Language Resource Center (NFLRC). The general direction of the Resource Center is set by a national advisory board. The Center conducts research, develops materials, and trains language professionals with the goal of improving foreign language instruction in the United States. The Center publishes research reports and teaching materials; it also sponsors a summer intensive teacher training institute. For additional information about Center programs, write

Dr. Richard Schmidt, Director
National Foreign Language Resource Center
1859 East-West Road #106
University of Hawai'i
Honolulu, HI 96822

or visit our Web site: http://www.lll.hawaii.edu/nflrc

NFLRC ADVISORY BOARD

CONTENTS

SECOND LANGUAGE DEVELOPMENT IN WRITING: MEASURES OF FLUENCY, ACCURACY, & COMPLEXITY

CHAPTER ONE

INTRODUCTION

In this report, we review the fluency, accuracy, and complexity measures that have been used in studies of second and foreign language development in written communication. The purpose of this review is to investigate two questions: 1) how is second language development in writing evaluated by these measures? and 2) which measures are the best indicators of developmental level in writing? In this search for the best measures, we compared the research results for more than a hundred measures of fluency, accuracy, or complexity that were used in thirty-nine second or foreign language research studies. The target languages included English and French as both second and foreign languages, Swedish as a second language, and German and Russian as foreign languages.

We will be focusing exclusively on studies that have looked at language development in written language. Although several studies have compared oral and written language (Hyltenstam, 1988, 1992; Larsen-Freeman, 1983; Scott & Tucker, 1974; Vann, 1979), and Bardovi-Harlig and Bofman (1989) have suggested that oral and written developmental data show comparable results, we are concentrating on measures of written language in order to ascertain where the results are clear in that domain alone. By focusing on writing alone, we can avoid having to wonder whether modality might be a confounding factor if the results are mixed for a particular developmental measure.

Because we want to measure language development in a communicative situation, we have attempted to include only the studies where writing is viewed as an act of communication, whether writing a narrative or persuasive essay (e.g., Perkins, 1980), writing a letter (e.g., Cumming & Mellow, 1996), describing a picture (e.g., Ishikawa, 1995), keeping a journal (e.g., Casanave, 1994), or responding to a film (e.g., Hyltenstam, 1988). We have also somewhat reservedly included the studies in which writers were asked to rewrite a simplified passage (e.g., Larsen-Freeman, 1983), partly because it has been done repeatedly since Hunt (1970) introduced the technique used by O'Donnell, Griffin, and Norris (1967). We have justified the inclusion of rewriting tasks to ourselves by viewing the rewriting task as an act of retelling that allows some choice in the manner of retelling, as evidenced by higher level planning than controlled sentence-combining tasks (Johnson, 1992). The key point is that we want to examine language development as it is manifest in written acts of communication, not in written form-focused exercises.

Furthermore, our primary purpose is to examine measures of language development, not language proficiency or writing proficiency per se. Language development refers

Wolfe-Quintero, K., Inagaki, S., & Kim, H.-Y. (1998). *Second language development in writing: Measures of fluency, accuracy, and complexity* (Technical Report #17). Honolulu: University of Hawai'i, Second Language Teaching and Curriculum Center.

to characteristics of a learner's output that reveal some point or stage along a developmental continuum. This includes developmental measures such as the number of clauses per T-unit, which are assumed to progress in a linear fashion as language use develops (Hunt, 1965). Language proficiency is a broader concept that is related to separating language users into cross-sectional groups based on a normal distribution of their language abilities. A language proficiency test includes a broad number of theoretically-motivated linguistic categories that can act as an overall gauge of language proficiency level (Bachman, 1990). Writing proficiency is a subset of language proficiency, with an emphasis on writing-specific abilities such as the production of a variety of genres and rhetorical features, but also including language-specific abilities such as the use of a range of vocabulary and syntactic structures. Writing proficiency measures are generally based on rating scales such as the holistic ACTFL (American Council on the Teaching of Foreign Languages) writing proficiency guidelines or the analytic scales proposed by Jacobs, Zinkgraf, Wormuth, Harfiel, and Hughey (1981).

Perkins (1983) has rightfully pointed out that developmental measures are not valid measures of writing proficiency. However, we are not interested in measuring the ability to 'write well' in a second language (e.g., Cumming, 1989), but in measuring language development as it is manifest in a written modality. Although many of the studies that have examined developmental measures have done statistical comparisons with language tests or writing proficiency rating scales, and although we will be considering these comparisons as part of our investigation, the constructs that they are measuring may be different.

THE SEARCH FOR A DEVELOPMENTAL INDEX

As Bardovi-Harlig & Bofman (1989) and Péry-Woodley (1991) point out, the second language acquisition literature contains two types of developmental studies: developmental sequence studies, which examine the acquisition orders for morphosyntactic features of language based on error and performance analysis; and developmental index studies, which attempt to gauge the development of learners at known proficiency levels through the use of fluency, accuracy, and complexity measures that are not necessarily tied to particular structures. Examples of the first type of study are the studies of morpheme acquisition order and the stages involved in the development of negation and relative clause acquisition. Examples of developmental index studies are those that measure certain features such as the length of error-free T-units, or the number of dependent clauses per total clauses in a language sample. In this research report, we will be reviewing only the developmental index studies. However, as the developmental index studies have expanded, hybrid ratio measures that look at particular structures have been created, including measures such as the correct pronoun uses per word (Evola, Mamer, & Lentz, 1980) and the number of passives per T-unit (Kameen, 1979).

The original goal of the developmental index studies begun in the late 1970s was the search for an index of development that could determine second language developmental level by means of an 'objective' measure. In first language acquisition, mean length of utterance (MLU) has commonly been used as a developmental index, but it doesn't work with adults who are cognitively mature (Larsen-Freeman & Strom, 1977). According to Larsen-Freeman (1983, p. 287), the goal was to find "a developmental yardstick against which global (i.e., not skill nor item specific) second language proficiency could be gauged." That yardstick should "increase uniformly and linearly as learners proceed towards full acquisition of a target language" (Larsen-Freeman, 1978, p. 440). Such a developmental index could be used by second language teachers and researchers who do not have access to the same language proficiency tests.

One important purpose of a developmental index would be to allow a more precise description of learners' developmental level in research studies. That would allow greater comparability between studies, perhaps comparability between developmental levels in different target languages (cf. Cooper, 1976; Harley & King, 1989; Hyltenstam, 1988; Monroe, 1975). However, no measure has emerged as a strong candidate; the results have been mixed for many of the most common measures considered. Consequently, Larsen-Freeman (1983, p. 301) suggested that it might be possible to use certain measures to ascertain a "gross estimate" of overall development, and then be able to use other measures that are more level appropriate to ascertain a more precise identification of developmental level. In a less ambitious goal, Ishikawa (1995, p. 66) indicated that she is not interested in finding an index of development, but would like to identify measures that relate to individual performance for learners at a very low proficiency level.

In second language acquisition research studies, developmental measures of fluency, accuracy, and complexity have also been used as dependent measures for examining the effect of a pedagogical treatment on either oral or written language use. That is, researchers have attempted to ascertain the effect of a particular instructional context by measuring differences on some of these developmental measures. They have been used in studies of the effect of program (Carlisle, 1989; Ferris & Politzer, 1981), feedback (Kepner, 1991; Robb, Ross, & Shortreed, 1986), task (Chastain, 1990; Foster & Skehan, 1996; Witte & Davis, 1983), grammar instruction (Frantzen, 1995), planning (Crookes, 1989; Foster & Skehan, 1996; Ortega, 1995), audience (Hirano, 1991), topic (Reid, 1992; Tapia, 1993; Tedick, 1990), and time (Kroll, 1990). The assumption is that these measures might be able to capture how the language use of learners differs in relationship to the context of use. Because developmental measures have been used by researchers in second language acquisition, it is important to examine the cumulative effect of the research that has attempted to show their relevance as indicators of language development.

FLUENCY, ACCURACY, AND COMPLEXITY

We have classified the measures that have been used in studies of second language development as belonging to three major categories corresponding to different aspects of development: a) fluency; b) accuracy; and c) complexity (both grammatical and lexical). This classification captures three types of intuitions that have been assumed in studies of second language development in writing:

1) Second language learners write more fluently, or write more in the same amount of time, as they become more proficient.

2) Second language learners write more accurately, or produce fewer errors in their writing, as they become more proficient.

3) Second language learners write more grammatically and lexically complex sentences as they become more proficient.

Most of the measures that have been used in the developmental index studies consist of intuitive rather than theoretical operationalizations of fluency, accuracy, and complexity. The underlying assumption is that these three characteristics of language development progress in tandem, that more proficient second language writers are more fluent, accurate, and complex in their writing than less proficient writers. However, some evidence suggests that there is individual variability at any given point of time, as well as points where one aspect of development may progress at the expense of another (i.e., there may be accuracy-complexity or accuracy-fluency trade-offs; see MacKay, 1982). For example, Casanave (1994) showed that learners vary in their patterns of T-unit length and accuracy in journal writing over time, and Tedick (1990) found that on field-specific compositions where writers took more risks and increased their T-unit length, the accuracy of those T-units decreased. Any assumptions of co-linear progression need to be investigated carefully (Young, 1995).

We are interested in finding fluency, accuracy, and complexity measures that work together to define a global picture of language development in second language writing. According to Lennon (1990, p. 390), in the traditional sense of these words, fluency refers to speaking with "native-like rapidity," accuracy refers to being "error-free," and complexity refers to "using a wide range of structures and vocabulary." These three components of development appear to correspond to two different aspects of language processing: language representation (also known as declarative knowledge, linguistic representation, usage, or competence) and language access (also known as procedural knowledge, access to or control of representations, use, or performance; see Bialystok, 1982). In this view, complexity and accuracy reflect the second language learner's current level of language knowledge; while complexity reveals the scope of expanding or restructured second language knowledge, accuracy shows the conformity of second language knowledge to target language norms. In comparison, fluency is a function of the control in accessing that knowledge, with control improving as the learner automatizes the process of gaining access.

In more recent theories of learning (Newell, 1990; Servan-Schrieber & Anderson, 1990), there have been suggestions that both representation and access are derived from how knowledge gets encoded (whether as instances, connections, or chunks; Schmidt, 1992). This possibility was first suggested by Newmark and Reibel (1968, p. 154), who claimed that adults are able "to infer general linguistic laws from particular instances." According to Ellis (1996), both language representation and language access arise from one learning process: the gradual strengthening of memories for language chunks. Ellis argued that memory for chunks is the source of all second language development, including phonology, grammar, lexis, and discourse, and including both automaticity and restructuring processes. According to Ellis, a better memory for chunks will result in better language learning, because there will be more language available for making the unconscious associations that are necessary for forming higher-level representations of knowledge. The stronger those representations are, the more available they will be for both restructuring and automatic access. When we measure fluency, we are measuring the observable outcome of automaticity of access, and when we measure accuracy or complexity, we are measuring the observable outcome of representation and restructuring.

In the search for developmental measures of fluency, accuracy, and complexity in writing, we want to investigate characteristics of writing that don't seem to be under a typical learner's conscious control, characteristics that may be indicators of language development as reflected in writing (such as the number of words produced per T-unit). Lennon (1990, p. 396) points out that there is a complex interconnection "between fluency, error, lexical range, syntactic complexity, and productivity," an interconnection that we feel is part of the process of a language learner attempting to encode many aspects of language at the same time, at many linguistic levels. The competition for attention and resources allows only so much information to be assimilated, automatized, or restructured at a time (Foster & Skehan, 1996). Whether or not this process is linear or nonlinear, continuous or discontinuous, remains to be seen.

It is also important to realize that the concepts of fluency, accuracy, and complexity can apply to different linguistic levels, including phonology, the lexicon, morphology, syntax, semantics, discourse, or pragmatics. For example, the learner's discourse abilities can be assessed in terms of how appropriate the discourse moves are in the context (accuracy), how varied the moves are (complexity), or how rapidly or easily the moves are executed (fluency). In this report we are going to focus our attention on the lexical, morphological, and syntactic aspects of writing development, because these have been the most heavily researched within second language writing, despite a number of interesting studies on other characteristics of writing, such as cognitive complexity (Shuqiang, 1987; Yau, 1991), topical structure (Schneider & Connor, 1991; Witte & Faigley, 1981), collocations (Dechert & Lennon, 1989), lexical error types (Zughoul, 1991), and lexical strategies (McClure, 1991). We are interested in morphological, syntactic, and lexical language development in writing rather than in characteristics of discourse or communication, although these are important areas of study.

THE RELATIONSHIP BETWEEN DEVELOPMENT
AND PROFICIENCY

One of the major goals of developmental index studies has been to compare developmental measures with an independent measure of language or writing proficiency by means of correlations, t-tests, or analysis of variance. The literature on language development in writing typically consists of cross-sectional studies which examine whether developmental measures can discriminate among these independently-determined proficiency levels. Although they are fewer in number, there are also some longitudinal studies which examine whether developmental measures can capture short-term progress in a typical class that is roughly at the same general proficiency level. The way in which proficiency is determined in each study may affect the results (Thomas, 1994), which poses a considerable challenge when we attempt to evaluate the utility of each developmental measure across different types of studies.

The variety of ways that language and writing proficiency have been conceptualized in the developmental index studies includes rating scales (e.g., Perkins, 1980), standardized tests (e.g., Vann, 1979), program levels (e.g., Larsen-Freeman, 1978), school levels (e.g., Yau, 1991), classroom grades (e.g., Kawata, 1991), short-term change in classes (e.g., Arthur, 1979), or comparisons with native speakers (e.g., Linnarud, 1986). These categories overlap with Thomas' (1994) identification of four general approaches to proficiency in current second language studies: impressionistic judgments, institutional status, in-house assessment, and standardized test scores. We need to distinguish between these methods of conceptualizing proficiency in order to allow for a direct comparison between studies in ways that may have influenced the results. For this purpose, in Appendix D we have subcategorized the studies based on the type of proficiency measure that was compared with the developmental measures that we are examining.

Each of these methods for defining proficiency level represents different conceptions of what constitutes language or writing proficiency. Holistic or analytic ratings are judgments about writing quality or writing proficiency, which may or may not overlap with judgments about language development, depending on scale goals. For example, some ratings are based on pass/fail judgments (Bardovi-Harlig & Bofman, 1989; Perkins, 1980), some ratings are based on traits such as communication or clarity (Fischer, 1984), and some are based on comprehensibility or overall ability (Kaczmarek, 1980). Standardized tests and program levels represent multi-trait assessment procedures that are focused on identifying levels of overall language proficiency, of which writing may be one part. Program levels and school levels are institutional constructs that may or may not represent actual proficiency level differences, particularly where placements are determined by a combination of test results and teacher judgments of level. Furthermore, holistic ratings and test scores can either be directly compared to developmental measures, or be used to define a set of proficiency levels which are then compared to developmental measures. Thomas (1994) argues that the latter practice can obscure results, particularly if the cut-off points between levels are arbitrary. Classroom grades given to writing samples can be influenced by a myriad of factors, including effort, length, number of errors, topic, number of sources, or whatever a particular teacher values. And longitudinal studies of classroom change vary in how samples are collected and compared over time. In other words, none of these methods of determining language or writing proficiency is directly comparable to any other.

Although the goal of developmental index studies has been to identify a linear relationship between measures of language development and measures of language or writing proficiency, Young (1995) has pointed out that we cannot assume that growth in language use is a linear or unitary process with various components of proficiency or development progressing at the same rate. However, if different components are measured independently (whether defined as aspects of reading/writing/listening/speaking, phonology/grammar/lexicon, or fluency/accuracy/complexity), it doesn't matter if they are multidimensional, develop at a different rate, or are context-dependent, so long as scores along each dimensional scale vary in a direct relationship with scores on the other scale in predictable ways in different contexts. Three types of comparisons are possible: comparisons between developmental measures and proficiency measures, comparisons among proficiency measures, or comparisons among developmental measures. The first two types of comparison have been done almost exclusively.

A comparison among measures is problematic only if growth in language use is nonlinear, perhaps because of a restructuring process (Young, 1995), or if there are gross discontinuities between any of the aspects of language use being measured. For measures of language proficiency, there may be learners who have very different abilities in oral versus literate modalities. For measures of language development, there may be writers who are fluent but inaccurate along with writers who are accurate but non-fluent, or writers with complex syntax but not a complex lexicon and vice versa (Hamp-Lyons, 1991). Even so, we feel that these potential nonlinear or discontinuous aspects of growth in language use can be identified through studies that attempt to correlate different types of measures with each other in a factor analysis. This has been done for measures of language proficiency such as scores on cloze tests or ratings for certain discourse features of oral interaction (e.g., Fouly, Bachman, & Cziko, 1990), but it has not been done for measures of fluency, accuracy, or complexity in language development.

Because the developmental index studies have been framed as a comparison of developmental measures to language or writing proficiency measures, we must begin with an analysis of their utility in that context. Consequently, we have developed specific criteria for representing how strongly a particular developmental measure discriminates among independently-determined proficiency levels (however they are determined). We have chosen to examine the results based on four levels of significance or correlation, as follows:

1) Developmental measures that highly correlate with proficiency (r=.65+) or show an overall effect for proficiency (p<.05) for three or more adjacent proficiency levels are represented with three stars (***) in our tables;

2) Developmental measures that moderately correlate with proficiency (r=.45–.64) or show an overall effect for proficiency (p<.05) for two or more proficiency levels are represented with two stars (**) in our tables;

3) Developmental measures that weakly correlate with proficiency (r=.25–.44) or show a trend towards an effect for proficiency (p<.10) are represented with one star (*) in our tables;

4) Developmental measures that show no correlation with or effect for proficiency are represented with an X in our tables.

Although we recognize that the same correlation may have a different level of significance depending on the particular study, this system allows us to roughly compare the relative strength of results for a particular measure across the relevant studies. We somewhat arbitrarily determined these levels of comparability partially based on Homburg (1984), who did both an analysis of variance and correlation analysis on the same set of data, and partially based on what seem like reasonably strong levels of correlation. For studies that don't report any statistics (Bardovi-Harlig, 1992; Casanave, 1994; Scott & Tucker, 1974), we evaluated the results as a trend if there was an obvious difference in the expected direction. Of course, this system is just a device, but it does provide a way of looking at potential effectiveness at a glance, with the understanding that the relationship is only broadly relative across studies. The hope is that a comparative investigation of these measures along many dimensions may reveal which ones are worth continuing to investigate and utilize in second language developmental research.

However, one problem with these comparisons is that they assume that developmental measures and proficiency measures are tapping into the same construct (concurrent validity), when that may not be so. Language development and language proficiency may be different constructs that should be measured in different ways. In order to demonstrate that a language proficiency test is testing the underlying construct 'proficiency,' it is necessary to decide independently what proficiency levels the groups are, and then see if the test discriminates in the expected ways. Likewise, in order to demonstrate that developmental measures are testing the underlying construct 'development,' it is necessary to determine developmental level independently. It is not altogether clear whether developmental level can be equated with proficiency level, or whether developmental level should be determined based on other aspects of known developmental stages.

We may not be far enough along in our understanding of developmental stages to be able to independently determine developmental level for a given writing sample. In first language studies using developmental measures, the independent measure of developmental level was widely-spaced age groups (Hunt, 1965), a criterion that can't be used in adult language learning. If developmental level and proficiency level are not the same construct, then the significance of the relationship between developmental measures and proficiency measures should not be the primary criterion for deciding whether a developmental measure is potentially useful. In fact, if the proficiency measure itself is not reliable (which can often be true for rating scales), then the likelihood of a developmental measure being significantly related to it is reduced (J. D. Brown, personal communication). Thus we should be careful before embracing or dismissing any developmental measure on the basis of the significance of its relationship to a proficiency measure.

Some studies have investigated whether measures of fluency, accuracy, or complexity can discriminate among existing program levels that encompass a broad range of language proficiencies (e.g., Larsen-Freeman, 1978), whereas other studies have investigated intact classes in which students are assumed to be at roughly the same proficiency level (e.g., Arthur, 1979). In these intact classes, the researchers have investigated whether developmental measures can discriminate among holistic ratings of the learners, or can indicate differences in language development over a relatively short period of time. Unfortunately, many developmental measures don't discriminate between adjacent program levels or among writing samples done in intact classes, presumably because the writing being compared is actually very similar developmentally. Likewise, when developmental measures have been used to examine the effects of a pedagogical treatment on development, the results have been mixed (e.g., Crookes, 1989; Foster & Skehan, 1996; Ortega, 1995), indicating that some of the measures may be too broad to capture anything other than large developmental differences.

Of all the types of proficiency measures, program level may be the most valid developmentally, if a variety of proficiency measures have been used to determine program level. In this investigation, we are assuming that if a fluency, accuracy, or complexity measure progresses linearly in a manner that is consistently identifiable with independently-determined proficiency levels across a variety of studies, and is also significantly related to program or school or test levels (although not necessarily to short-term change in classes or holistic ratings or comparisons with native speakers), it is a good candidate for a developmental measure.

CALCULATING FLUENCY, ACCURACY, AND COMPLEXITY MEASURES

Although we have characterized developmental measures as measures of fluency, accuracy, and complexity, we can further characterize measures by considering the method by which they are calculated. The first type of calculation is a simple frequency count of a particular feature, structure, or unit. For example, researchers have counted the number of words, clauses, or T-units in a writing sample to obtain a frequency score. Frequency measures are problematic because they vary as a function of the amount of time allotted to the writer or the nature of the task. Although placing limits on a task conceptually (rewriting a passage, describing a picture) or temporally (writing a composition within a fixed time limit) can yield writing that is comparable using absolute frequencies, the results are meaningless in comparison with other populations or across different tasks.

A more valid type of calculation is a ratio measure, in which the presence of one type of unit is expressed as a percentage of another type of unit, or one type of unit is divided by the total number of comparable units (e.g., error-free units per total units of the same type). Ratios can be used to measure the length of a given unit (e.g., words per clause, sentence or T-unit), the rate of accuracy within a given unit (e.g., errors or error-free units per clause, sentence or T-unit), or the complexity of a given unit (e.g., clauses per T-unit, or T-units per sentence). In some studies, the researchers multiplied their ratio or index figure by 100 to yield a percentage, but that type of difference in calculation is ignored in this comparison between studies, because it doesn't change either the relative score on the measure or the fundamental method of calculation.

A third type of calculation is an index based on a formula that yields a numerical score. Such indices generally are developed either when the researcher determines that the features being examined belong to a weighted hierarchy of complexity or sophistication (e.g., Flahive & Snow, 1980; Perkins, 1980), or the researcher wants to use a more complex formula than a simple ratio to calculate a score (e.g., Bardovi-Harlig, 1992). One example is the Error Index developed by Kaczmarek (1980), which is defined as the number of error-free words minus the number of errors divided by the number of error-free words. Each index has its own formula (see Appendices 1 and 2 for lists of measures both by type and alphabetically, along with their method of calculation).

In this report, we haven't worried about the different ways that measures were labeled within different studies. Rather, we extrapolated from the authors' discussions the actual formula used in the calculation in order to compare measures that were calculated in the same way, regardless of what the measures were called by the authors. We have labeled the measures with a name and a symbol, with the symbol being a representation of the method of calculation. For example, frequency counts of the number of clauses (C), T-units (T), or error-free T-units (EFT) are referred to by a symbol with no mathematical formula. Ratio counts such as the subordination ratio (C/T) can be calculated by dividing the number of clauses by the total number of T-units. Formulas are more difficult to represent, so their name is their symbol.

The reliability and validity of the method of calculation of the developmental measures is also important for determining their usefulness as indicators of development, but this has rarely been examined or reported. Of the thirty-nine studies examined here, only seven reported interrater or intrarater reliability correlations for their developmental measure scoring procedures (Bardovi-Harlig, 1992; Bardovi-Harlig & Bofman, 1989; Cummings & Mellow, 1996; Gipps & Ewen, 1974; Ishikawa, 1996; Tapia, 1993; Tedick, 1990). Even when correlations between raters have been reported, little information has been provided on how judgments were made, or where areas of disagreement occurred, which reduces replicability (Polio, 1997). Polio also points out that for accuracy measures, it is one thing to achieve close agreement on the total number of error-free T-units in a composition, but quite another to achieve agreement on the accuracy of each individual T-unit. Unlike most studies, Polio reports rates for both overall and specific agreement on accuracy judgments, as well as precisely how units were defined and where there were areas of difficulty in achieving agreement.

There also needs to be an indication of the reliability of the proficiency measures that are used as a basis of comparison with the developmental measures, particularly for judgments on rating scales or in-house proficiency tests. Out of sixteen studies that used holistic rating scales, only eight reported interrater or intrarater reliability correlations on the scoring procedure (Arthur, 1979; Engber, 1995; Fischer, 1994; Flahive & Snow, 1980; Henry, 1996; Homburg, 1984; Larsen-Freeman & Strom, 1977; Tedick, 1990). Only Larsen-Freeman (1983) reported reliability figures for an in-house placement test used to establish program levels.

With respect to validity, we are looking for measures that repeatedly tap into the construct 'development' regardless of how well they correlate with the measures of language proficiency that have been used. For example, if a developmental measure shows a linear progression across proficiency levels in studies that define proficiency in very different ways, that may support the construct validity of that measure even though the results may have been significant for only some of the studies (J. D. Brown, personal communication). The consistency of the results for a developmental measure over many studies with different subjects also suggests that there is repeated measures reliability, which may be more valuable than the internal reliability of a single test (Thom Hudson, personal communication). Another important factor is the concurrent validity of developmental measures when they are significantly related to or highly correlated with certain measures of proficiency such as independently-determined program levels. These issues will be addressed as we consider what the best developmental measures of fluency, accuracy, and complexity may be.

THIS REPORT

In this report, there are five main chapters followed by extensive appendices. In chapters 2 through 5, we will examine the studies within four categories of measures: fluency, accuracy, grammatical complexity, and lexical complexity. Within each of these chapters, we will look at the frequency, ratio, and index measures that have been utilized by researchers investigating second language writing. Summary charts that compare measures of the same type are presented in each chapter, followed by a detailed look at the individual measures and studies. In chapter 6, we will consider the issues surrounding a determination of the best measures of second language development.

There are also six appendices that summarize the studies in various ways. Appendix A is a list of the measures that we are investigating, their type, how each is calculated, and the code we are using to refer to the measure. Appendix B is an alphabetical list of the codes and calculations to aid in looking up the measures. Appendix C is a summary of the key features of the language development studies, including the first and second languages involved, how proficiency levels were defined, how the writing samples were collected, what measures were investigated, and what statistical tests were performed. Appendix D is a summary of the results by study (in alphabetical order), which looks at how the measures fared based on our rating system. Appendix E is a summary which breaks down the results based on the type of language or writing proficiency measure that was used as a basis of comparison — whether it measured learners in the same class or at different levels, and whether proficiency was defined as short-term change in intact classes, holistic or analytic ratings of writing samples, placement tests, program level, school level, or grades. Appendix F is a summary of the results by developmental measure, bringing together the summary charts scattered throughout the report, so that the relative effectiveness of each measure can be ascertained at a glance.

Some research articles reported more than one study, as in Larsen-Freeman (1983), which contained two studies of written data (as well as an oral study), including one that is cross-sectional and one that is longitudinal, each involving different populations of learners. These individual studies will be referred to as 'study 1,' 'study 2,' and so forth, as in Larsen-Freeman (1983: study 1). In addition, within each study, occasionally the subjects completed more than one task, as in Larsen-Freeman (1983: study 2), in which the same subjects rewrote a passage and then wrote an essay on a given topic. These individual tasks will be referred to as 'task 1' or 'task 2,' as in Larsen-Freeman (1983: study 2–task 1). In some studies, researchers performed more than one type of analysis of the same data, which will be referred to as 'analysis 1' and 'analysis 2,' as in Flahive and Snow (1980: analysis 1). And finally, some researchers performed their analyses on separate groups, which will be referred to here as 'group 1' or 'group 2,' as in Ishikawa (1995: analysis 1–group 2), or on different levels, as in Flahive and Snow (1980: analysis 2-level 5). The numbering will generally follow the order that the studies, tasks, analyses, groups, and levels are presented in the original article.

The ultimate goal of this investigation is to determine which developmental measures have been most successful thus far in representing second language development in writing, which are the most promising for further investigation or suggest other potential measures, and which seem the most reliable and valid across studies and methods of comparison, at a meta-level of analysis.

CHAPTER TWO

THE FLUENCY MEASURES

Fluency measures reveal how comfortable the second language writer is with producing language. Part of language development is the ease with which the language user can retrieve the language items that he or she needs, which can vary for native speakers and language learners depending on context and abilities (Lennon, 1990). Fluency is "the processing of language in real time" (Schmidt, 1992, p. 358) with a focus on "the primacy of meaning" (Foster & Skehan, 1996, p. 304); hence, it is related to the production pressures that a language user faces while communicating a message in either writing or speech. Fluency can also involve the appropriate use of routines, whether the routine is a pragmatic formula (House, 1996), or an automatized chunk of language (Ellis, 1996). The use of routines will result in an increase on measures of fluency, because the units of production will be longer and easier to produce within a given time frame.

However, there can be confusion when the term fluency is used, because of the various ways it has been defined. Fillmore (1979) discussed fluent speakers in terms of how fast they talk, how coherent and complex their speech is, whether the speech is appropriate, and how creative it is. The same can be said for second language writers, who may be considered fluent if they can produce written language rapidly, coherently, appropriately, and creatively. However, as Fillmore acknowledged, this is a somewhat vague characterization, because it encompasses complexity and accuracy as well as discourse-related criteria.

Another characterization of fluency is automaticity of language use. According to Towell, Hawkins, and Bazergui (1996, p. 85), "fluent second language production requires that knowledge (from whatever source) be proceduralized." Schmidt (1992, p. 358) also characterized fluency as an "automatic procedural skill" that is relatively free from conscious attention, and which may be developed through learning mechanisms such as the encoding of instances into memory (Logan, 1988), the strengthening of connections between stimuli and responses (Cohen, Dunbar, & McClelland, 1990), or the chunking of sequences into higher-level patterns (Ellis, 1996; Newell, 1990; Servan-Schreiber & Anderson, 1990). Schmidt contrasted this with the traditional view that language development is the "increasingly skillful application of abstract rules" (1992, p. 377), arguing that what appear to be rules in learners' language may be sophisticated applications of memory retrieval, strengthening, or chunking, and that these result in automaticity in processing, and thus fluency in language use.

Lennon (1990) used the term 'fluency' in a more narrow sense to mean only rate and length of output. In his view, oral fluency measures are of two types: those that measure temporal aspects, such as words per minute or pause length; and those that measure dysfluency, such as repetitions and false starts. These measures indicate how successful the speaker is in coping with real time processing and in keeping up with the interaction. Although researchers have been concerned with fluency in the analysis of oral discourse more than in the analysis of written communication, the equivalent to the temporal variables in oral discourse would be length and rate measures of written production.

We have decided to restrict our measurement of fluency to issues of rate and length. In our view, fluency means that more words and more structures are accessed in a limited time, whereas a lack of fluency means that only a few words or structures are accessed. Learners who have the same number of productive vocabulary items or productive structures may retrieve them with differing degrees of efficiency. Fluency is not a measure of how sophisticated or accurate the words or structures are, but a measure of the sheer number of words or structural units a writer is able to include in their writing within a particular period of time.

The primary way to measure fluency is to count the number, length, or rate of production units. Production units include sentences, T-units, clauses, and phrases. For example, one marker of fluency is the length of a composition in timed writing, as Larsen-Freeman (1978) pointed out: "Subjects with a higher proficiency tended to write longer compositions — perhaps because of their fluency" (p. 444). Fluency can also be measured by considering the length of production units by counting the average number of words contained in them. It is plausible to consider measures of the length of sentences, T-units, or clauses in writing as similar to measures of the length of pause-bound utterances in speaking (Crookes, 1990). Another way to measure fluency is to consider the rate of production, which in writing is the number of words per minute (Arthur, 1979), but in speech is either the number of words per minute (Lennon, 1990) or syllables per second (Griffiths, 1991; Ortega, 1995). If writing is done under timed conditions, the sheer number of words written becomes a rate measure.

Length measures, such as words per T-unit (W/T) or utterance (W/U), have traditionally been considered measures of complexity, because longer production units are assumed to indicate the presence of more complex structures. However, we disagree with this assumption, and consider all length measures to be measures of fluency, because length measures "do not discriminate between the various ways length can be achieved" (O'Donnell, 1976, p. 33; Cooper, 1976; Yau, 1991). The association of length measures with fluency was also suggested by Ortega (1995) in her study of the speech of 32 learners. In a factor analysis, Ortega found that length (words per utterance) was strongly related to rate (syllables per second), and that both were part of one factor presumed to be fluency, but not related to factors associated with lexical complexity or grammatical accuracy.

We have also included two other fluency measures that may appear to be related more to complexity than to fluency, including the average length of complex nominals in T-units (measured as the number of words in complex nominals per

T-unit, or WCN/T), and the average length of complex nominals per clause (measured as the number of words in complex nominals per clause, or WCN/C) (Yau, 1991). Although the use of complex nominals is clearly related to complexity of language use, these measures don't capture that. They merely measure how fluent (how long) the complex nominals are, not how prevalent they are in the writing sample, nor the sources of the complexity. In our view, these measures capture the likelihood that as writers become more fluent, the length of their nominals increases. A better approach to capturing how complex the nominals are would be to count the number of complex nominals per total nominals (CN/N), per clauses (CN/C), or per T-units (CN/T). Cooper (1976) used the latter measure which will be discussed later.

We have also chosen to consider several 'error-free' measures to be fluency measures because they essentially capture the fluency of a writer within the context of writing accurate sentences. These are measures of the total number of words within error-free T-units (WEFT) or words within error-free clauses (WEFC), as well as the average number of words per error-free T-unit (W/EFT) or words per error-free clause (W/EFC). Although words per error-free T-unit (W/EFT) has been considered a complexity measure just as words per T-unit (W/T) has, these error-free length measures reveal the degree of fluency of the error-free T-units or clauses, but don't reveal the degree of accuracy itself. Ishikawa (1995) supports this interpretation when she contrasts measures of quantity (length) with quality (error), stating "to consider both kinds of measures 'syntactic' is to miss the very real distinction between them" (p. 56). For example, one writer may produce only one accurate T-unit that happens to be very long. That writer will have a higher score on words in error-free T-units (WEFT) or words per error-free T-unit (W/EFT) than another writer who produces many more accurate T-units that are shorter on average. The first writer is more fluent in an accuracy context, as the words per error-free T-unit measure would indicate, but the second writer is more accurate overall, something that is not captured by these measures.

In our view, the crucial issue in classifying types of ratio measures is what is contained in the numerator of the measure. In the measure W/T (the number of words per T-unit), the numerator is the number of words, and that represents length, or fluency. In the measure EFT/T (the number of error-free T-units per T-unit), the numerator is the number of error-free T-units, and that represents accuracy. In the measure CN/T (the number of complex nominals per T-unit), the numerator is the number of complex nominals, and that represents complexity. The denominator indicates only the context for the measure (the production unit), not the type of measure it is. Future studies should consider doing factor analyses to determine the relationship between these measures in language use.

FLUENCY FREQUENCIES

For fluency frequency measures, most of the studies examining the frequency of occurrence of a particular production unit (e.g., words, clauses, sentences, or T-units) have not shown any significant difference between groups. The most noteworthy significant result has been for total number of words (W), although even there the results have been mixed, as shown in Table 1 below. The significant effect for words is most evident in studies that compared learners at different proficiency levels. However, the validity of any of these as measures of fluency is doubtful, both because of the clear lack of results, and because of the lack of a fixed delimiter as found in ratio measures.

Table 1. Fluency frequencies: Number of studies by type of result

measure	code	***	**	*	X
words	W		10	1	7
verbs	V		1		
clauses	C				3
sentences	S				6
T-units	T		1	3	8
words in T-units	WT				2
words in clauses	WC				2
words in error-free T-units	WEFT	1	1	1	2
words in error-free clauses	WEFC		1		1

*** Developmental measures that highly correlate with proficiency (r=.65+), or show an overall effect for proficiency (p<.05) together with a significant difference between three or more adjacent proficiency levels (p<.05).

** Developmental measures that moderately correlate with proficiency (r=.45–.64), or show an overall effect for proficiency for two or more proficiency levels (p<.05).

* Developmental measures that weakly correlate with proficiency (r=.25–.44), or show a trend towards an effect for proficiency (p<.10).

X Developmental measures that show no correlation with or effect for proficiency.

Words (W)
W = total number of words

***	
**	Hirano 91: analysis 2; Homburg 84: analysis 1; Kameen 79; Larsen-Freeman 78; Larsen-Freeman 83: study 2–task 1, task 2, study 3; Linnarud 86: analysis 1, analysis 2; Tedick 90
*	Hirano 91: analysis 1
X	Henry 96; Ishikawa 95: analysis 1–group 1, group 2; Kawata 92; Nihalani 81; Perkins 80; Tapia 93

Many researchers have counted the number of words in a text as a measure of the overall fluency of the writing. It is clear, however, that number of words is not a reliable measure of development, because of the mixed results. Ten studies found a significant difference in number of words, and one a trend towards difference, while seven found no difference at all. Nine of the studies that showed a trend or significant effect compared writers at different proficiency levels using a composition with a time limit (Hirano, 1991: analysis 1, analysis 2; Homburg, 1984: analysis 1; Kameen, 1979; Larsen-Freeman, 1978; Larsen-Freeman, 1983: study 2–task 1, task 2; Linnarud, 1986: analysis 1; Tedick, 1990). One other was a longitudinal study of changes in an intact class (Larsen-Freeman, 1983: study 3); although the effect in Larsen-Freeman varied based on the particular assignment, one of which was a take-home paper.

Notably, all of the studies that found no significant difference (except Henry, 1996) investigated learners that were roughly at the same proficiency level (Ishikawa, 1995: analysis 1–group 1, group 2; Kawata, 1992; Nihalani, 1981; Perkins, 1980; Tapia, 1993). Although Tapia (1993) used two adjacent program levels (out of seven), she found that in holistic ratings that there was no significant difference between the levels, which may explain why there was no difference in the developmental measures either. Larsen-Freeman (1978, 1983) also pointed out that this measure can show a ceiling effect with the number of words 'clustering' or even decreasing at advanced levels, which is what Henry (1996) found.

Verbs (V)
V = total number of verbs

***	
**	Harley & King 89
*	
X	

In a comparison of native and second-language sixth graders in a French immersion program, Harley and King (1989) found that the native students used significantly more verbs (V) in timed compositions than the second language students did. Presumably, it is because they wrote more, as Harley and King acknowledged, but they didn't report composition lengths. Whether this measure can discriminate between second language groups has not been established.

Clauses (C)
C = total number of clauses

***	
**	
*	
X	Ishikawa 95: analysis 1–group 1, group 2; Kameen 79

Neither of the two studies that used number of clauses (C) as a measure found a significant effect for proficiency, with Ishikawa (1995: analysis 1) comparing beginning-level students' writing before and after a three-month interval, and Kameen (1979) comparing 'good' and 'poor' written samples based on holistic ratings.

Sentences (S)

S = total number of sentences	
***	
**	
*	
X	Homburg 84: analysis 1; Ishikawa 95: analysis 1–group 1, group 2; Kameen 79; Kawata 92; Perkins 80

Although six studies examined the number of sentences (S) as a potential factor in identifying proficiency differences, none of them found a significant effect. If there is no real difference in the number of sentences in compositions, it may be because learners of low proficiency can produce simple sentences while learners of high proficiency can produce more complex sentences. Presumably, measures that probe the internal characteristics of sentences will be more useful in differentiating these learners than a simple count of the number of sentences. It should be noted that Hunt (1965) abandoned counting the number of sentences in children's writing because there was often a lack of punctuation and a preponderance of run-on clauses joined by *and*. However, Bardovi-Harlig (1992) argued that the sentence may be a relevant unit for examining the complexity found in adult second language learners' writing because of its psychological reality for both teachers and learners.

T-units (T)

T = total number of T-units	
***	
**	Ishikawa 95: analysis 1–group 1
*	Tomita 90: analysis 1-level 1, level 2, level 3
X	Hirano 91: analysis 1; Homburg 84: analysis 1; Ishikawa 95: analysis 1–group 2; Kameen 79; Kawata 92; Perkins 80; Tedick 90; Tomita 90: analysis 2

A T-unit is defined as "one main clause plus the subordinate clauses attached to or embedded within it" (Hunt, 1965, p. 49). Hunt used the T-unit as a measure of the minimal terminable unit of language, that is, the smallest unit that could be considered a grammatical sentence, whether it was punctuated that way by the writer or not. As these studies indicate, the total number of T-units in a written sample is not a good fluency measure because eight studies found no significant difference based on number of T-units, while Tomita (1990) found a trend towards a difference for three school levels, and only Ishikawa (1995) found a significant difference, but only for one of two beginning-level groups. It appears that the overall number of T-units may actually decrease with increased proficiency, as T-units increase in length.

Words in T-units (WT)

WT = total number of words in T-units	
***	
**	
*	
X	Ishikawa 95: analysis 1–group 1, group 2

Ishikawa (1995) measured the total number of words that were found in T-units (WT). This measure has only been used by Ishikawa, who was searching for measures that would be relevant to the writing of beginning level students. She counted only T-units that were contained in student-marked sentences, not allowing T-units to cross student-marked boundaries (following Homburg, 1984, but unlike Hunt, 1965). She did not count fragments or exclamations as either T-units or clauses. Ishikawa found that the number of words in T-units were different from the number of total words in the written text. However, just as she found for the overall word measure, Ishikawa found no significant difference in number of words in T-units between picture descriptions written three months apart.

Words in clauses (WC)

WC = total number of words in clauses	
***	
**	
*	
X	Ishikawa 95: analysis 1–group 1, group 2

Ishikawa (1995) is also the only one who measured the total number of words that were found in clauses (WC). She did not count fragments or exclamations as clauses. Ishikawa found that the number of words in clauses were different from the number of total words in the written text. However, like the overall word measure, she found no significant difference in the number of words in clauses for picture descriptions written three months apart by beginning learners.

Words in error-free T-units (WEFT)

WEFT = total number of words in all error-free T-units	
***	Hirano 91: analysis 2
**	Perkins 80
*	Hirano 91: analysis 1
X	Ishikawa 95: analysis 1–group 1, group 2

What does counting the number of words present in error-free T-units (WEFT) display about language development? Presumably, the number of words in error-free T-units increases as learners use longer sentences with more accuracy; however, it is quite easy to imagine that a beginning learner who writes very simple sentences might be able to produce more accurate T-units than someone who is taking greater risks with longer, more complex T-units. The latter case would result in many more words per T-unit in general, but perhaps a low percentage of accurate T-units, and hence a low count of words contained in those T-units. Furthermore, because it is not a ratio measure, in order for the total number of words in error-free T-units (WEFT) to be useful, a time limit must be set in order to control for equivalence across compositions that are being compared.

The words in error-free T-units (WEFT) measure has had mixed results in studies that have employed it. Perkins (1980), but not Hirano (1991: analysis 1), found that words in error-free T-units was related to test scores, Hirano (1991: analysis 2) found that words in error-free T-units was related to program levels, but Ishikawa (1995) found that there was no difference in words in error-free T-units for beginning-level writers after three months of instruction. Thus, the number of words in error-free T-units may be more relevant for distinguishing different proficiency levels rather than identifying short-term gains by a group at a similar proficiency level.

The general interpretation in the literature has been that words in error-free T-units (WEFT) is primarily an accuracy measure, but it is our opinion that this is a variant of any measure that counts words, which we are treating as fluency measures because we believe that length is the primary indicator of fluency. In this measure, the count happens to occur in an accuracy context, so it tells us how fluent the accurate T-units are. However, this measure does not tell us how many words or T-units are wrong or right, which would be the accuracy measures EFW (the number of error-free words) or EFT (the number of error-free T-units); the words in error-free T-units measure tells us only how many words occurred in accurate strings.

Like other frequency measures, the words in error-free T-units (WEFT) measure doesn't take into account the total number of T-units from which the error-free T-units were drawn, nor the total number of words from which the words in error-free T-units were drawn. In order to represent the length of error-free T-units in a manner that is comparable across compositions and studies, it would be better to use a fluency ratio such as W/EFT (the number of words per total error-free T-units). If a comparable representation of accuracy is the goal, it would be better to use the accuracy ratios EFW/W (the number of error-free words per total words) or EFT/T (the number of error-free T-units per T-unit). These latter measures capture the relationship between words, T-units, and error in ratios that can be compared across studies. These measures will be discussed in the relevant sections.

Words in error-free clauses (WEFC)

WEFC = total number of words in all error-free clauses

***	
**	Ishikawa 95: analysis 1–group 1
*	
X	Ishikawa 95: analysis 1–group 2

Only Ishikawa (1995) has employed the words in error-free clauses (WEFC) measure, which is a variant of the words in error-free T-units (WEFT) measure discussed above. Her motivation for counting the number of words in error-free clauses was to limit how long the error-free string had to be for the words to be countable, because her subjects were beginners. It is easier to make an error in a T-unit, which can contain many clauses, than it is to make an error in a single clause. However, Ishikawa found that only one of the two beginning-level groups significantly improved on this measure after three months of instruction.

FLUENCY RATIOS

Fluency ratios are much more successful than frequencies in distinguishing between proficiency levels/indicating language development. Although Table 2 shows somewhat mixed results for many of the measures, particularly for two of the most often-used measures, length of T-units (W/T), and length of error-free T-units (W/EFT), a closer analysis of the results reveals that when the average length of production units such as clauses, sentences, T-units, or error-free T-units is calculated, there is a strong relationship to proficiency, with a gradual increase in length as proficiency develops. However, these measures tend to be related to more global differences between proficiency levels rather than to the finer differences found within a single proficiency level or intact class.

Table 2. Fluency ratios: Number of studies by type of result

measure	code	***	**	*	X
words per minute	W/M		2		
clause length	W/C		5	1	3
sentence length	W/S		5		5
T-unit length	W/T	4	19	5	12
error-free T-unit length	W/EFT	2	13	2	9
error-free clause length	W/EFC	1			2
complex nominal length per T-unit	WCN/T		1		
complex nominal length per clause	WCN/C		1		

*** Developmental measures that highly correlate with proficiency (r=.65+), or show an overall effect for proficiency (p<.05) together with a significant difference between three or more adjacent proficiency levels (p<.05).

** Developmental measures that moderately correlate with proficiency (r=.45–.64), or show an overall effect for proficiency for two or more proficiency levels (p<.05).

* Developmental measures that weakly correlate with proficiency (r=.25–.44), or show a trend towards an effect for proficiency (p<.10).

X Developmental measures that show no correlation with or effect for proficiency.

Words per minute (W/M)

W/M = total number of words divided by total number of minutes	
***	
**	Arthur 79: study 1, study 2
*	
X	

Words per minute (W/M) is a measure of writing speed that was used in only one study (Arthur, 1979) as an indicator of fluency and articulateness. This measure corresponds to the common use of rate measures in studies of oral fluency. In the first study reported in Arthur (1979), a significant difference was found for words per minute on compositions written at two points in an ESL composition class (5.84 words per minute at time one; 7.02 words per minute at time two). In the second study, writing speed was found to be the most significant factor in a discriminant analysis relating the measures to a holistic rank ordering of essays by teachers.

Clause length (W/C)

W/C = total number of words divided by total number of clauses

***	
**	Cooper 76; Hirano 91: analysis 2; Kameen 79; Monroe 75; Yau 91
*	Hirano 91: analysis 1
X	Ishikawa 95: analysis 1–group 1, group 2; Sharma 80

Clause length, or number of words per clause (W/C), has some empirical support as a measure of writing fluency, beginning with Hunt (1965). Clause length tends to gradually increase at each proficiency level and has been shown to discriminate among non-adjacent school levels (Cooper, 1976; Monroe, 1975; Yau, 1991), as well as between non-adjacent program levels (Hirano, 1991: analysis 2) and two groups separated by holistic ratings (Kameen, 1979). However, Hirano (1991: analysis 1) and Sharma (1980) found no relationship between clause length and test scores, and Ishikawa (1995) found no significant difference in clause length after three months of instruction for beginning-level students. However, a comparison of the means across studies shows that there is a range from 5.20 words per clause for the lowest level learners to 10.83 for the most advanced, and that words per clause increases in a linear relationship to proficiency regardless of whether the results were significant or not. Ishikawa (1995) suggested that clauses may be a much better method for examining beginning-level learners than the T-unit, which may only be appropriate for learners who have already attained a certain degree of proficiency in the target language (Gaies, 1980; Homburg, 1984).

Sentence length (W/S)

W/S = total number of words divided by total number of sentences

***	
**	Cooper 76; Homburg 84: analysis 1, analysis 2; Kameen 79; Monroe 75
*	
X	Ishikawa 95: analysis 1–group 1, group 2; Kawata 92; Linnarud 86: analysis 1, analysis 2

Empirical studies indicate that sentence length, or words per sentence (W/S), tends to discriminate among nonadjacent program or school levels (Cooper, 1976; Monroe, 1975) and between holistic ratings (Homburg, 1984: analysis 1; Kameen, 1979 [but not Linnarud, 1986]). Homburg (1984: analysis 2) also found in a discriminant analysis that sentence length was the strongest factor for differentiating among holistic ratings. However, sentence length does not seem to be a useful measure for discriminating between periods of time (Ishikawa, 1995) or among grades (Kawata, 1992).

Increases in the number of words per sentence (W/S) can capture the degree to which run-on or coordinated sentences have been produced, and a high ratio can indicate problems in punctuation rather than fluency per se. In fact, this was the motivation for Hunt (1965) to develop T-units as an alternative to sentences, because younger children struggled with punctuation. Hunt also pointed out that the words per sentence (W/S) measure mathematically consists of two developmentally conflicting measures: words per T-unit (W/T), which tends to go up with increasing proficiency, and T-units per sentence (T/S), which tends to go down with increasing proficiency (yielding the following formula: W/T x T/S = W/S). This makes it more difficult for the words per sentence measure to discriminate between developmental levels, since longer sentences can arise either from a more immature writer who overuses coordinated and run-on sentences, or from a more mature writer who has increased the length of his or her T-units.

A comparison of the means across studies shows that there is a range from 8.5 words per sentence for the lowest level learners (estimated from Kawata's Table 3, p. 51) to 23.59 for the most advanced, with words per sentence increasing in a linear relationship to proficiency in most studies. However, Homburg (1984) found that those with a score of 7 out of 10 on a holistic rating scale used fewer words per sentence (21.33) than those with a score of 6 out of 10 (23.59).

T-unit length (W/T)

W/T = total number of words divided by total number of T-units

***	Flahive & Snow 80: analysis 1; analysis 2-level 6; Hirano 91: analysis 2; Larsen-Freeman 83: study 2–task 1
**	Cooper 76; Flahive & Snow 80: analysis 2-level 4, level 5; Gipps & Ewen 74; Henry 96; Hirano 91: analysis 1; Homburg 84: analysis 1; Ho-Peng 83: task 1, task 2; Ishikawa 95: analysis 1–group 1; Kameen 79; Kawata 92; Larsen-Freeman 78; Larsen-Freeman 83: study 2–task 2, study 3; Monroe 75; Tedick 90; Tomita 90: analysis 2; Yau 91
*	Arnaud 92; Casanave 94; Flahive & Snow 80: analysis 2-level 2, level 3; Tomita 90: analysis 1-level 2
X	Arthur 79: study 1, study 2; Flahive & Snow 80: analysis 2-level 1; Ishikawa 95: analysis 1–group 2; Larsen-Freeman & Strom 77; Nihalani 81; Perkins 80; Sharma, 80; Tomita 90: analysis 1-level 1, level 3; Vann 79: analysis 1, analysis 2

Hunt (1965) originally found that T-unit length, or the number of words per T-unit (W/T), was the best measure for representing first language development in writing, because it showed the highest percentage of gain from age group to age group. T-unit length has also been one of the most often used measures of second language development, and it has turned out to be significant for 23 studies, but not significant for 17 studies, although 5 of them showed a trend towards a significant difference. T-unit length seems to discriminate best when there is a wide range of proficiency levels, either based on program placement (Hirano, 1991: analysis 2; Ho-Peng, 1983: task 1, task 2; Larsen-Freeman, 1978, 1983: study 2–task 1, task 2; Tedick, 1990), school level (Cooper, 1976; Gipps & Ewen, 1974; Henry, 1996;

Monroe, 1975; Tomita, 1990: analysis 2; Yau, 1991), or standardized test score (Hirano, 1991: analysis 1). There are more mixed results when the range of proficiency levels are being rated holistically (non-significant results: Larsen-Freeman & Strom, 1977; Vann, 1979: analysis 2; significant results: Homburg, 1984: analysis 1; Kameen, 1979). In other studies, Vann (1979: analysis 1) found that words per T-unit did not account for the variance in TOEFL scores, and Arthur (1979: analysis 2) found that words per T-unit did not relate to a holistic rank ordering of compositions.

These results suggest that the T-unit length measure (W/T) is related to broad distinctions between program or school levels, but not as clearly to holistic ratings or other proficiency measures. However, a comparison of the means across studies shows that there is a range from 6.0 words per T-unit for the lowest level learners to 23.0 for the most advanced, with words per T-unit increasing in a linear relationship with proficiency, regardless of how proficiency was measured or whether the results were significant. This repeated sampling reliability of the linear nature of the words per T-unit measure across studies suggests that it may be a very useful measure indeed.

Most researchers have treated T-unit length as a measure of grammatical complexity, but we disagree with this analysis. As Cooper (1976) states, "there are two possible ways to account for this increase in [T-unit] length: (1) a writer can add more dependent clauses to the T-unit and (2) a writer can lengthen the existing clauses by adding phrases and words" (p. 177). This is based on Hunt (1965), who showed that words per T-unit (W/T) equals the number of words per clause (W/C) times the number of clauses per T-unit (C/T; the formula is W/C x C/T = W/T. Accordingly, words per T-unit can increase either through longer clauses or more subordinate clauses. Arthur (1979) also points out that T-units can be lengthened by the ellipsis of repeated elements in coordinated sentences, which is not a particularly sophisticated way to increase the number of words per T-unit.

Because the words per T-unit (W/T) measure doesn't distinguish between causes of increasing length, some of which are more grammatically complex than others, we believe that it is primarily a fluency measure. Counting the number of words per T-unit only directly measures length, not complexity, and we are treating length as the primary component of fluency. Certainly, using T-units as the production unit confuses matters, because T-units include complexity as part of their definition. A more direct measure of fluency would be to count the number of words per clause (W/C), because that would remove the influence related to whether the clauses are main or subordinate, which is a complexity issue. A more direct measure of complexity would be to avoid length altogether and count the number of subordinate or dependent clauses as a ratio to overall clauses. Those measures will be discussed in the section on grammatical complexity.

Error-free T-unit length (W/EFT)

W/EFT = total number of words in error-free T-units divided by total number of error-free T-units

***	Hirano 91: analysis 2; Kawata 92
**	Arnaud 92; Hirano 91: analysis 1; Ho-Peng 83: task 1, task 2; Larsen-Freeman 78; Larsen-Freeman 83: study 2–task 1, task 2, study 3; Sharma 80; Tedick 90; Tomita 90: analysis 1-level 3; Vann 79: analysis 1, analysis 2
*	Casanave 94; Tomita 90: analysis 1-level 1
X	Arthur 79: study 1, study 2; Ishikawa 95: analysis 1–group 1, group 2; Perkins & Leahy 80: analysis 1, analysis 2; Tapia 93; Tomita 90: analysis 1-level 2, analysis 2

The length of error-free T-units, which is calculated as the number of words per error-free T-unit (W/EFT), is a measure that has been used extensively in second language studies ever since Larsen-Freeman (1978) reported significant results, and it has turned out to be a somewhat useful measure of second language proficiency, with 16 studies finding a significant relationship between error-free T-unit length and other measures of proficiency, and 11 studies finding no difference, although two showed a trend towards difference. Of these latter studies, nine compared learners within intact classes (Arthur, 1979: study 1, study 2; Casanave, 1994; Ishikawa, 1995: analysis 1–group 1, group 2; Perkins & Leahy, 1980: analysis 1, analysis 2; Tomita, 1990: analysis 1-level 1, level 2), and one compared learners who were rated the same on a holistic measure (Tapia, 1993), suggesting that this measure is not appropriate for discriminating among learners in the same class or at the same level, although the ratio of words per error-free T-unit did progress linearly even in the non-significant studies. However, in an analysis of individual learners' journal entries, Casanave (1994) found that some learners vacillated in words per error-free T-unit over three semesters. Since the conditions for writing journal entries can vary in both time allotted and the topic written about, this is not particularly surprising.

Furthermore, of the 15 studies finding a significant relationship, 10 of them contained more than two proficiency levels, although only Hirano (1991: analysis 2) and Kawata (1992) found a significant difference in words per error-free T-unit for three or more adjacent proficiency levels. Presumably this is because change in this factor is so gradual, which confirms that words per error-free T-unit is a measure that is useful for discriminating among learners at very different proficiency levels, but not between those in the same class or at nearly the same level. In discriminant analyses, Vann (1979) found that words per error-free T-unit (W/EFT) and error-free T-units per T-unit (EFT/T) accounted for the most variance in TOEFL scores, but Arthur (1979) did not find a connection between words per error-free T-unit and a rank ordering of compositions. A comparison of the means across studies shows that there is a range from 3.80 words per error-free T-unit for the lowest level learners to 16.91 for the most advanced, although the latter average length was obtained on take-home essays (Perkins & Leahy, 1980). The subjects in Larsen-Freeman (1983: study 3) had an average words per error-free T-unit score of 16.15 for their take-home paper. The longest average words per error-free T-unit ratio for a timed composition was 12.2 (Tapia, 1993). Scores on words per error-free T-unit do appear to progress in a linear relationship to proficiency.

The assumption behind measuring error-free T-unit length is that learners will be able to write longer T-units that are accurate as they progress in overall proficiency, and based on the results of these studies, that assumption seems warranted. However, a majority of these researchers have considered words per error-free T-unit an accuracy measure, because the concept of 'error-free' is involved. Again, we disagree with this analysis, and are treating this measure as a fluency measure rather than an accuracy measure, because it measures the average length of error-free T-units, not the number or degree of accuracy of those units (cf. Ishikawa, 1995). This measure tells us how fluent the error-free T-units are, but not how many there are or how accurate the composition is. True measures of accuracy are EFT (the number of error-free T-units) or EFT/T (the number of error-free T-units per total T-units), both of which will be discussed in the section on accuracy.

Error-free clause length (W/EFC)
W/EFC = total number of words in error-free clauses divided by total number of error-free clauses

***	Ishikawa 95: analysis 2
**	
*	
X	Ishikawa 95: analysis 1 – group 1, group 2

Only Ishikawa (1995) has employed the error-free clause length measure (the number of words per error-free clause; W/EFC), which is a variant of the error-free T-unit length measure (W/EFT) discussed above. Her motivation for counting the average number of words in error-free clauses was to limit how long the error-free string had to be for the words to be countable, because her subjects were beginners. It is easier to make an error in a T-unit, which can contain many clauses, than it is to make an error in a single clause. However, Ishikawa found that neither of her two beginning-level groups significantly improved on this measure after three months of instruction. A comparison of the means in these analyses shows that for these low level learners, there was a range from 3.95 to 4.84 words per error-free clause.

Interestingly, in her second analysis, Ishikawa found that the number of words per error-free clause (W/EFC) correlated strongly with the summed Z-scores of 24 measures for both the pre- and post-tests of both groups. However, a glance at the means for words per error-free clause reveals that the reason for this high correlation is that this measure is very similar across all four tests and has low variability. This means that although the score is highly reliable and representative (her second analysis), it indicates nothing about growth in writing development (her first analysis). Like words per error-free T-unit (W/EFT), this measure does not detect change within intact classes, but should be investigated further for its utility in distinguishing broad proficiency levels.

Complex nominal length per T-unit (WCN/T)

WCN/T = total number of words in complex nominals divided by total number of T-units

***	
**	Yau 91
*	
X	

Yau (1991) examined the average length of complex nominals in T-units, or the number of words in complex nominals per T-unit (WCN/T), and found that it successfully discriminated between the writing of first and second language ninth graders and second language freshmen in college in Hong Kong. A comparison of the means in this study shows that the ESL ninth graders had 2.37 words in complex nominals per T-unit, whereas the native language ninth graders had 6.71. The ESL thirteenth graders had 6.00 words in complex nominals per T-unit, placing them near the native language ninth graders. Yau (1991, pp. 271–272) defined 'complex nominals' as headed nominals that were expanded by restrictive modifiers of all types, including adjectives, relative clauses, and prepositional or participial phrases, as well as non-headed nominals such as that-clauses or infinitive phrases. She claimed that the increased use of complex nominals is a marker of developmental maturity, following Mellon (1979), who claimed that a slow rise in restrictive modification was a "direct and unavoidable consequence of the development of conceptual knowledge" (p. 18).

Although the use of complex nominals may be a matter of complexity of language use, this particular measure doesn't capture that. It is a measure of how fluent (how long) the complex nominals are, not how prevalent they are in the writing sample. This is a fluency measure in a complexity context. This measure captures the likelihood that as writers become more fluent, the length of their nominal modifications increases. Since Hunt (1965) originally found that the frequency of complex nominals increased with developmental age, we feel that a more straightforward measure of the complexity associated with the presence of complex nominals would be to count the number of complex nominals per total nominals (CN/N) or per total T-units (CN/T). The latter measure was used by Cooper (1976) and will be discussed in the chapter on grammatical complexity.

Complex nominal length per clause (WCN/C)

WCN/C = total number of words in complex nominals divided by total number of clauses

***	
**	Yau 91
*	
X	

Yau (1991) also examined the ratio of words in complex nominals to clauses (WCN/C), and found it just as discriminating as the ratio of words in complex nominals to T-units (WCN/T). A comparison of the means in this study shows that the ESL ninth graders had 1.72 words in complex nominals per clause, whereas the native language ninth graders had 3.80. The ESL thirteenth graders had 4.09 words in complex nominals per clause, which means that they were better than the younger native speakers. This measure captures the likelihood that as writers become more fluent, the length of their nominal modifications increases, although it is subject to the same criticisms as the measure of the number of words in complex nominals per T-unit (WCN/T) that was discussed above.

CONCLUSION: FLUENCY MEASURES

The best measures of fluency appear to be three ratio measures. Two of them are based on the T-unit as the production unit, and they are T-unit length (W/T) and error-free T-unit length (W/EFT). The other one is based on the clause as the production unit, and it is clause length (W/C). These three measures consistently increased in a linear relationship to proficiency level across studies, regardless of task, target language, significance of the results, or how proficiency was defined. The consistent and linear nature of these measures is shown in the Table 3 showing the mean ratios in studies that used timed essays or rewriting tasks, and in which proficiency level was defined as either a program level, school level, or holistic rating applied to learners across a wide range of proficiency levels. The only exception was in Larsen-Freeman, 1983, where W/EFT declined at the upper level (marked by "†").

Table 3: Comparison of means on fluency measures across studies that examine multiple program or school levels

Timed essay, proficiency = program or school level			
study/levels	W/T	W/C	W/EFT
Cooper, 1976			
sophomores	10.3	7.3	
juniors	12.6	7.4	
seniors	15.2	8.5	
graduates	16.9	9.9	
natives	23.0	10.7	
Flahive & Snow, 1980			
level 1	7.00		
level 2	8.71		
level 3	10.89		
level 4	12.24		
level 5	12.63		
level 6	13.56		
Henry, 1996			
semester 1	5.1		
semester 2	5.3		
semester 4	6.2		
semester 6	7.3		
Hirano, 1991			
low	8.88	7.28	5.95
mid	10.00	7.44	7.64
high	12.64	8.33	9.38
Ho-Peng, 1983			
level 1	13.40		7.74
level 2	16.26		13.64
level 3	16.47		16.01
Larsen-Freeman, 1978			
level 1	12.02		4.61
level 2	13.72		7.52
level 3	15.23		9.26
level 4	15.25		10.77
level 5	15.67		13.20

continued…

Timed essay, proficiency = program or school level			
study/levels	W/T	W/C	W/EFT
Larsen-Freeman, 1983			
level 2	13.73		8.36
level 3	17.11		12.61
level 4	17.21		11.36[†]
Tapia, 1993			
level 5	10.0		
level 6	11.1		
Tedick, 1990			
beginning	12.53		9.54
intermediate	13.70		11.16
advanced	15.50		11.46
Tomita, 1990			
grade 10	6.43		5.56
grade 11	6.76		5.85
grade 12	7.17		6.16
Yau, 1991			
ESL grade 9	10.82	7.62	
ESL grade 13	15.54	10.48	
Rewriting task, proficiency = program or school level			
Ho-Peng, 1983			
level 1	9.01		7.84
level 2	9.81		9.03
level 3	11.12		11.08
Larsen-Freeman, 1983			
level 1	6.22		5.64
level 2	7.45		7.55
level 3	9.34		8.43
level 4	9.95		9.34
Monroe, 1976			
freshmen	6.78	5.64	
sophomores	8.42	5.79	
juniors/seniors	9.38	6.21	
graduates	10.98	7.28	
natives	13.23	7.94	

continued…

Table 3: Comparison of means on fluency measures across studies that examine multiple program or school levels (cont.)

Timed essay, proficiency = program or school level			
study/levels	W/T	W/C	W/EFT
Sharma, 1980			
low intermediate	9.31	6.44	6.06
high intermediate	9.86	6.97	8.41
advanced	10.26	7.48	9.49
Timed essay, proficiency = holistic rating of range of levels			
Homburg, 1984			
rating 5	10.99		
rating 6	14.28		
rating 7	15.00		
Kameen, 1979			
'poor'	14.30	8.54	
'good'	18.40	10.83	
Larsen-Freeman & Strom, 1977			
'poor'	11.58		
'fair'	12.50		
'average'	12.92		
'good'	14.28		
'excellent'	14.46		

† The only instance in which W/EFT declined at the upper level

For these three fluency measures, there was more likely to be a significant relationship between the developmental measure and the proficiency measure when proficiency was defined as a program or school level rather than as a holistic rating or short-term change in an intact class. In most cases, even if there was overall significance, there wasn't a significant difference between adjacent levels. However, because of the reliable and consistent linear relationship between these three fluency measures and proficiency level, we feel that they have construct validity as measures of language development.

CHAPTER THREE

THE ACCURACY MEASURES

Foster and Skehan (1996) defined accuracy as "freedom from error," which can be measured by an analysis of target-like use, taking into account both the contexts and uses of the structure in question (Pica, 1983). Thus, accuracy is the ability to be free from errors while using language to communicate in either writing or speech. However, Thomas (1994, p. 328) criticized measures that are based on a comparison with the target language, preferring measures that analyze the interlanguage as a system. We feel that grammatical and lexical complexity measures do analyze the interlanguage system, and that the purpose of accuracy measures is precisely the comparison with target-like use. Whether that comparison reveals or obscures something about language development is another question.

We believe that accuracy in language use can arise from three interacting sources: the degree of accuracy of the language representation itself, the strength of competing representations, and the degree of automatization of language production. When a learner encodes the target language in the process of language learning, each aspect of the learner's representation may approximate the target language system to varying degrees. Furthermore, each aspect of the representation can vary in how strongly or automatically it gets retrieved when activated. According to MacKay (1982), when (language) production is still in the process of being automatized, there are trade-offs between speed and accuracy, such that there are more errors when production is either extremely slow or extremely rapid. There are also more errors when there is interference from extraneous representations, particularly if they are both closely-related and stronger in their activation. This opens up the possibility that in second language development, representations of the first language or earlier stages of the second language may overwhelm production of newer, more tentative representations. However, as more correct representations get strengthened over time, they will be more likely to get activated.

MacKay (1982) also pointed out that once production is fully automatized, there tend to be fewer errors. However, in second language learning, if the representation is faulty but access is fully automatized, it may lead to production that is error-full but impervious to change (perhaps the source of what has been called fossilization). When MacKay (1982) claimed that there are fewer errors in automatized production, what that means is that there is a closer match between the underlying system and production, because production is automatic. If the underlying system is problematic, that can be a source of second language error.

The crucial issue is then how automatic and impervious to change the underlying representations are. If they are still in the process of being strengthened, there is room for restructuring of the knowledge so that it conforms more closely to the input. McLaughlin (1990) argued that greater automaticity of lower-level knowledge can free up resources for the restructuring of higher-level knowledge. Ellis (1996) also claimed that memory for chunks is the basis of not only automaticity and fluency, but also the higher-level restructuring that can result in complexity or accuracy gains. Once language knowledge gets encoded by a learner, it may then be automatized in access (leading to greater fluency), or restructured in representation (leading to greater complexity or accuracy). When the restructuring of language knowledge results in greater accuracy, that gain in knowledge may or may not be consciously recognized by the learner. As Schmidt (1990) pointed out, attention, but not necessarily conscious awareness, may be crucial for learning.

Brumfit (1984) offered a pedagogical contrast between accuracy and fluency. In his view, accuracy is an explicit display of language usage for evaluation, whereas fluency is an implicit and automatic use of natural language for communication. For him, the important issue is whether classroom attention gets allocated to learning accurate target language forms to achieve accuracy, or to communicating a message to achieve fluency. In this view, accuracy is the outcome of a conscious attention to form, rather than the outcome of an unconscious restructuring process. However, we think that accuracy can encompass both of these points of view, because accuracy can be related to a continuum from more implicit to more explicit forms of language knowledge.

Of course, a more explicit or conscious access to certain aspects of language knowledge can play a role in the self-monitoring of language production, including the conscious editing of writing. We feel that the conscious application of editing knowledge in writing is part of the higher level control over plans (Schmidt, 1992) that exists in all language production. Editing is a conscious plan, but the language choices made while editing are subject to the same gradual development of automaticity and restructuring as all language knowledge is. As Schmidt (1992) pointed out, errors themselves may be automatized, and a language learner may not even be aware of an error in his or her writing despite conscious attention to the writing. One well-known phenomenon in writing pedagogy is the automatic self-correction of low-level errors that occurs when basic writers read their writing out loud (Bartholomae, 1980), as well as the difficulty with other types of errors even when conscious attention is allocated to editing (Zamel, 1995). Writers are dependent on the state of their language knowledge when it comes to the types of errors they search for, notice, or are able to correct, either automatically or through a conscious struggle.

Error has always been an important issue in the analysis of second language development. The fundamental assumption is that as writers become more proficient, it becomes easier for them to produce increasingly accurate language. It was pointed out by Gaies (1976) and Larsen-Freeman (1978) that structural errors in second language learners' writing, like the use of oversimplified sentence structures, are an indication of "incomplete syntactic control" (Gaies, 1976, cited in Larsen-

Freeman, 1978, p. 445). A lack of knowledge of the second language can manifest itself as simplification (the complexity issue) or as error (the accuracy issue).

One assumption about language development is that the development of accuracy (fewer errors) goes hand-in-hand with an increase in fluency (faster rate and greater length) and an increase in complexity (more lexical and grammatical variety). However, there may be trade-offs between complexity, fluency and accuracy; the more complex sentences learners try to produce, the more errors they may be likely to make (Foster & Skehan, 1996), and the more rapidly they produce language that isn't fully automatic, the more errors they may be likely to make (MacKay, 1982). Tedick (1990), who studied the effect of prior knowledge of a topic on writing, found that on a more specific topic second language writers produced longer T-units, but that fewer of those T-units were error-free. Greater error may be a factor in the risk-taking associated with creating longer T-units. However, this trade-off may be a factor only at certain points in time; complexity and accuracy may progress together over long-term development.

A developmental analysis of the accuracy of a second language writer involves counting the errors in a text in some fashion, and two approaches to this process have been developed. One approach has been to focus on whether a structural unit of some type is error-free, whether clauses, sentences, or T-units. Typical measures found in this approach are the number of error-free T-units per T-unit (EFT/T) or the number of error-free clauses per clause (EFC/C). In determining whether production units such as the T-unit or clause are error-free, a decision has to be made about what counts as an error. The decision to include or exclude various types of errors depends on the learners' level, the discriminative value of the errors within the population, and the researcher's preferences.

For example, Larsen-Freeman and Strom (1977), Larsen-Freeman (1978, 1983), Henry (1996), Hirano (1991), and Sharma (1980) counted morphosyntactic, lexical, spelling, and even punctuation errors when determining if a T-unit was error-free. Homburg (1984) counted all of these except punctuation errors. In contrast, Scott and Tucker (1974) and Arnaud (1992) counted only morphosyntactic errors, while Vann (1979) and Casanave (1994) counted morphosyntactic and lexical errors, and Ishikawa (1995) counted morphosyntactic, lexical, and discourse errors. Not everyone investigating error-free T-units specified what they counted as an error (Arthur, 1979; Kawata, 1992; Perkins, 1980; Perkins & Leahy, 1980; Tapia, 1993). These differences between criteria for determining 'error-free' would certainly affect the results, making it difficult to interpret the meaningfulness of comparisons across studies.

Error-free measures were criticized by Bardovi-Harlig and Bofman (1989, p. 22), who pointed out that measures such as error-free T-units per T-unit do not reveal how errors are distributed within the T-unit (or any other unit of analysis), because a T-unit containing a single error is treated identically to a T-unit containing multiple errors. In addition, error-free measures do not reveal what types of errors are involved, because all types of errors that are being analyzed are treated as equivalent for purposes of determining the correctness of a unit. This merely suggests that error-free measures may not be sufficient by themselves to reveal how accurate a composition is, which is why Gaies (1980) argued for the development of a hierarchy of error types.

Because of these criticisms of error-free T-unit measures, researchers such as Arthur (1979), Bardovi-Harlig and Bofman (1989), and Homburg (1984) have developed a second approach, which is the analysis of how many errors occur in relation to production units such as words, clauses, or T-units. This approach is not concerned with identifying strings of error-free language, only quantities of errors. In this approach, all errors can be considered, as in the calculation of the number of errors per word (E/W), or errors of various types can be considered, as in the calculation of morphological errors per clause (MorE/C). Errors can classified as syntactic, morphological, lexical, or semantic, or classified based on some other method, such as Homburg's (1984) division into first, second, and third-degree errors, or Zughoul's (1991) analysis of different lexical error types. Again, for those who counted the total number of errors, there are differences in what they considered to be an error. For example, Homburg (1984) and Linnarud (1986) counted morphosyntactic, lexical, and spelling errors, but Flahive and Snow (1980), Perkins (1980), and Perkins and Leahy (1980) didn't specify what constituted an error in their studies.

While these different taxonomies are informative about potential error types, it would be more helpful if theoretical criteria were developed for determining either the type or gravity of errors. In most of these studies, the determination of errors seems to be based primarily on the researcher's intuitions, intuitions which seem to vary from study to study. Because of the inconsistencies that he noted, Gaies (1980) argued that there was a need for incorporating an error hierarchy into analyses of error-free T-units. If a classification of errors were based upon an explicit model of what constitutes syntactic or lexical knowledge, then errors could be classified in a more principled manner. A related approach to classifying errors is to determine how grave particular errors are, as Homburg (1984) did in his classification of errors as first-, second-, or third-degree. However, these types of judgments are quite subjective, and error gravity research in general suffers from many problems in comparability (Rifkin & Roberts, 1995).

The classification of error type may make it possible to identify errors and potential developmental patterns in a more precise manner. For example, although Larsen-Freeman and Strom (1977) found that the ratio of error-free T-units to overall T-units increased by proficiency level, when they looked at particular error types, they found that errors in prepositions did not decrease while errors in verb tense did, and that errors in articles increased from level 1 to level 2, remained the same at level 3, and then decreased at levels 4 and 5. In an unpublished study by Neuman (1977, cited in Larsen-Freeman & Strom, 1978, p. 127), she found that the beginning level learners made the most errors in word order, but that the advanced learners made more errors than the intermediate level, which is an example of an inverted developmental U. This suggests that the relationship between error and proficiency level may be non-linear in variable ways. In fact, if errors of different types show different linear and non-linear patterns, we may be led to conclude that any analysis of errors in general won't discriminate between developmental levels, and that their use should be abandoned. The inclusion of multiple error types may make any measure of general error too coarse, including such measures as errors per T-unit (E/T) or error-free T-units per T-unit (EFT/T).

However, the non-linear results for particular error types may be an artifact of the analysis, and with a better analysis, a developmental progression may become more obvious. For example, little is known about a developmental progression in the acquisition of prepositions or verb tense, and what we do know about article acquisition is that definite and indefinite articles may develop at different times (Huebner, 1983). Since these types of error analyses have not been tied to finely-tuned information about developmental stages, the results should be viewed cautiously.

From another point of view, Evola et al. (1980) and Cumming and Mellow (1996) looked at correctness, not errors, when they compared ratios of correct uses of particular morphemes to words or to contexts. Examples include the calculation of the number of correct pronouns per word (CorrPN/W), or the number of correct definite article uses per required or supplied context (CorrDEF/CX). The best example of this is Cumming and Mellow (1996), who examined the target-like use of morphemes known to follow a certain developmental path: plurals, then definite articles, then indefinite articles, then third-person singular. Although they weren't able to completely support the developmental claims, their analysis was theoretically motivated. In studies like this, the distinction between the developmental sequence and developmental index studies is blurred, because the goals have merged to produce developmental measures that are tied to known stages of development. Indeed, we need more sophisticated ways to measure the language use in writing in developmental terms — not to measure language use directly against target language norms, but against well-established developmental sequences (such as those related to morphemes, negatives, questions, and relative clauses).

ACCURACY FREQUENCIES

For the accuracy frequency measures, the most noteworthy significant results have been for the total number of error-free T-units (EFT), as shown in Table 4 below. The significant effect for error-free T-units is most evident in studies that compared learners at different proficiency levels on timed compositions, although some of the findings (Sharma, 1990; Tomita, 1990) suggest that the relationship between error-free T-units and proficiency may be non-linear. Other potentially interesting findings are that an overall error count (E) may correlate with holistic ratings (Linnarud, 1986: analysis 2; Perkins, 1980), and a particular type of serious but comprehensible error ('second-degree' errors) may be also be related to holistic ratings (Homburg, 1984: analysis 1). However, most of the studies examining the frequency of occurrence of particular error types (e.g., first-degree errors, correct pronouns) have not shown any significant difference between groups. In general, the validity of frequency measures of accuracy is doubtful because of the lack of a fixed denominator as found in ratio measures.

Table 4. Accuracy frequencies: Number of studies by type of result

measure	code	***	**	*	X
error-free T-units	EFT	3	10		3
error-free clauses	EFC	1	1		1
errors	E		1	1	1
first-degree errors	1DE				1
second-degree errors	2DE		1		
third-degree errors	3DE				1
correct connectors	CorrCN			1	
correct pronouns	CorrPN			1	
correct articles	CorrART			1	

*** Developmental measures that highly correlate with proficiency (r=.65+), or show an overall effect for proficiency (p<.05) together with a significant difference between three or more adjacent proficiency levels (p<.05).

** Developmental measures that moderately correlate with proficiency (r=.45–.64), or show an overall effect for proficiency for two or more proficiency levels (p<.05).

* Developmental measures that weakly correlate with proficiency (r=.25–.44), or show a trend towards an effect for proficiency (p<.10).

X Developmental measures that show no correlation with or effect for proficiency.

Error-free T-units (EFT)
EFT = total number of error-free T-units

***	Hirano 91: analysis 2; Tomita 90: analysis 1-level 1, analysis 1-level 2
**	Hirano 91: analysis 1; Homburg 84: analysis 1, analysis 2; Ishikawa 95: analysis 1–group 1; Perkins 80; Perkins & Leahy 80: analysis 1; Sharma 80; Tedick 90; Tomita 90: analysis 1-level 3, analysis 2
*	
X	Ishikawa 95: analysis 1–group 2; Kawata 92; Perkins & Leahy 80: analysis 2

The number of error-free T-units (EFT) appears to discriminate among proficiency levels. Thirteen studies found a significant relationship between error-free T-units and proficiency as measured by program level (Hirano, 1991: analysis 2; Sharma, 1980; Tedick, 1990), standardized test scores (Hirano, 1991: analysis 1), holistic ratings (Homburg, 1984: analysis 1, analysis 2; Perkins, 1980), grades (Tomita,

1990: analysis 1-level 1, level 2, level 3, analysis 2), comparison with native speakers (Perkins & Leahy, 1980: analysis 1) or instruction (Ishikawa, 1995: analysis 1–group 1). Only three studies did not, with two of them comparing error-free T-units with grades (Kawata, 1992; Perkins & Leahy, 1980: analysis 2), and with change after exposure to instruction in general (Ishikawa, 1995: analysis 1–group 2).

As with other frequency measures, in order for error-free T-units to be useful, a time limit must be set. This was done in most of the studies, but not in Perkins and Leahy (1980), who gave a take-home essay assignment, and found a non-significant relationship between proficiency and error-free T-units. One way to control for length of the sample would be to look at error-free T-units per T-unit (EFT/T), per sentence (EFT/S), or per word (EFT/W), measures that will be discussed in the next section on accuracy ratios.

The number of error-free T-units is expected to increase as proficiency increases. However, this assumption may be false, since there may be a trade-off between accuracy and complexity that prevents a co-linear relationship. In fact, Tomita (1990) found that among high school students studying English in Japan, the number of error-free T-units increased from the first to the second year, but decreased from the second to third year. Tomita (1990, p. 24–25) suggested that the third-year students committed more errors because they tried to write longer and more complex sentences. Sharma (1980) found the reverse curve with university-level learners: the number of error-free T-units decreased from low intermediate to high intermediate learners, and then increased for the advanced learners. Tomita's subjects were likely to be less advanced than Sharma's, and perhaps his advanced learners were like Sharma's intermediate learners.

Considering these two studies together leads to the tantalizing hypothesis that the relationship between error-free T-units and proficiency is a zigzag, with an early increase in correctness followed by a decrease and then a later increase (in something like an italicized N shape). Note that the U shape commonly associated with accuracy in language development has been identified for particular phenomena such as past tense morphology, whereas the error-free T-unit ratio measure is more global in scope and may follow a different path. A decrease in error-free T-units might also correlate with an increase in complexity, although this comparison has not been investigated directly by anyone.

Error-free clauses (EFC)
EFC = total number of error-free clauses

***	Ishikawa 95: analysis 2
**	Ishikawa 95: analysis 1–group 1
*	
X	Ishikawa 95: analysis 1–group 2

Only Ishikawa (1995) employed an EFC measure (the number of error-free clauses), which is a variant of the error-free T-unit (EFT) measure discussed above. Her motivation for counting the number of error-free clauses was to limit how long the error-free string had to be, because her subjects were beginners. It is easier to make an error in a T-unit, which can contain many clauses, than it is to make an error in a single clause. However, Ishikawa found that only one of the two beginning-level groups significantly improved on this measure after three months of instruction (analysis 1), although the measure proved to be highly reliable when correlated with the summed Z-scores of 24 measures for both the pre- and post-tests of both groups (analysis 2).

Errors (E)

E = total number of errors	
***	
**	Perkins 80
*	Linnarud 86: analysis 2
X	Homburg 84: analysis 1

All three of these studies examined the number of errors (E) found in timed compositions. Both Perkins (1980) and Linnarud (1986) compared the number of errors to holistic ratings of the compositions, and Perkins found a significant effect for overall errors, while Linnarud found a trend towards a difference but Homburg (1984: analysis 1) did not find a significant relationship between them. One way to control for length would be to look at the number of errors per T-unit (E/T), errors per word (E/W) or errors per clause (E/C), measures that will be discussed in the next section on accuracy ratios.

First-degree errors (1DE)

1DE = total number of first-degree errors (completely understandable)	
***	
**	
*	
X	Homburg 84: analysis 1

Homburg (1984: analysis 1) analyzed various types of errors based on their gravity, following Nas (1975). He looked at what he calls 'first-degree' errors (1DE), which include minor deviations in spelling, meaning, register, or grammatical form that do not interfere with understanding of the text at all. He found no significant difference between holistic ratings for these types of errors.

Second-degree errors (2DE)

2DE = total number of second-degree errors (understandable from context)

***	
**	Homburg 84: analysis 1
*	
X	

Homburg (1984: analysis 1) also examined what he calls 'second-degree' errors (2DE), which include serious deviations in spelling, meaning, grammatical form, or word order that are still interpretable within the context of the text, despite their seriousness. For these types of errors, he found a significant difference between holistic ratings. However, as he recognizes, this classification is quite subjective; thus its utility as a measure of second language development is doubtful.

Third-degree errors (3DE)

3DE = total number of third-degree errors (interferes with understanding)

***	
**	
*	
X	Homburg 84: analysis 1

Homburg (1984: analysis 1) also examined what he calls 'third-degree' errors (3DE), which include serious deviations in form or meaning that completely interfere with the comprehensibility of the text. For these types of errors, he found no significant difference between holistic ratings.

Correct connectors (CorrCN)

CorrCN = total number of connectors used correctly

***	
**	
*	Evola et al. 80: analysis 2
X	

Evola et al. (1980: analysis 2) compared holistic ratings with the number of connectors used correctly (CorrCN) in essays written by learners at different proficiency levels. They found only a trend towards significance.

Correct pronouns (CorrPN)

CorrPN = total number of pronouns used correctly	
***	
**	
*	Evola et al. 80: analysis 2
X	

Evola et al. (1980: analysis 2) also compared holistic ratings with the number of pronouns used correctly (CorrPN) in essays written by learners at different proficiency levels. Again, they found only a trend towards significance.

Correct articles (CorrART)

CorrART = total number of pronouns used correctly	
***	
**	
*	Evola et al. 80: analysis 2
X	

Evola et al. (1980: analysis 2) also compared holistic ratings with the number of articles used correctly (CorrART) in essays written by learners at different proficiency levels. They found only a trend towards significance.

ACCURACY RATIOS

Table 5 presents the results for the various accuracy ratios that have been used in studies of second language writing development. As can be seen in the table, many of the measures have been used in only one or two studies, though two of the measures, the error-free T-unit ratio (EFT/T) and the errors per T-unit ratio (E/T), have been used in quite a few studies, albeit with contradictory findings. Researchers have tended to prefer only one of these two methods for examining errors, but a comparison of these two measures in future studies would be useful.

A closer analysis of the results reveals that error-free T-units per T-unit (EFT/T) does not capture changes in accuracy for short-term studies within intact classes, and has mixed results for program levels. It's possible that error-free T-units per T-unit may be a non-linear measure, as results from Larsen-Freeman (1983) and Tomita (1990) suggest. Furthermore, the errors per T-unit (E/T) measure appears to correlate with holistic ratings but not program proficiency levels, indicating that errors are part of what teachers pay attention to in making their judgments. Research on holistic ratings as an assessment tool confirms that there is a strong correlation between errors and holistic ratings (Sweedler-Brown, 1993), although trained raters have also been shown to ignore errors (Carlisle & McKenna, 1991). It may depend on the individual rater's orientation to errors (Vaughan, 1991; Perkins, 1983; Henry, 1996).

Other notable results include the significant results for the error-free clauses per sentence (EFC/S) measure developed by Ishikawa (1995) to examine the growth in writing of beginning-level students over a three-month period. Homburg's (1980) analysis of 'second-degree' errors per T-unit (2DE/T) suggests that errors that are serious but do not interfere with communication correlate with holistic ratings. However, determining error gravity would need validation of interrater reliability, and is fraught with problems (Rifkin & Roberts, 1995). Another interesting proposal is Bardovi-Harlig and Bofman's (1989) use of clauses rather than T-units as the basic measure of error analysis, in order to eliminate complexity as a factor. They found that an advanced group of learners made more morphological errors per clause (MorE/C) than lexical errors (LexE/C), but that the lexical errors correlated best with a pass/fail judgment. Of course, most of these measures need a great deal of further study.

Table 5. Accuracy ratios: Number of studies by type of result

measure	code	***	**	*	X
error-free T-unit ratio	EFT/T	4	8	3	8
error-free T-units per sentence	EFT/S		2		2
error-free T-units per word	EFT/W				1
error-free sentence ratio	EFS/S				1
error-free clause ratio	EFC/C		1		2
error-free clauses per sentence	EFC/S	1	2		
error-free clauses per t-unit	EFC/T		1		1
words in error-free clauses ratio	WEFC/WC		1		1
errors per T-unit	E/T		6	2	3
first-degree errors per T-unit	1DE/T				1
second-degree errors per T-unit	2DE/T		1	1	
third-degree errors per T-unit	3DE/T				1
errors per clause	E/C	1		1	1
syntactic errors per clause	SynE/C				1
morphological errors per clause	MorE/C			1	
lexical errors per clause	LexE/C		1		
verb lexical errors per verb	VLexE/V		1		

continued...

Table 5. Accuracy ratios: Number of studies by type of result (cont.)

measure	code	***	**	*	X
lexical errors per lexical word	LexE/LW			1	
errors per word	E/W	1	1		
grammatical errors per word	GrE/W	1	1	1	1
semantic errors per error	SemE/E				2
correct connectors per word	CorrCN/W				1
correct pronouns per word	CorrPN/W				1
correct article ratio	CorrART/CX		2		1
correct definite article ratio	CorrDEF/CX		1		1
correct indefinite article ratio	CorrINDEF/CX	1		1	
correct plural ratio	CorrPL/CX				2

*** Developmental measures that highly correlate with proficiency (r=.65+), or show an overall effect for proficiency (p<.05) together with a significant difference between three or more adjacent proficiency levels (p<.05).

** Developmental measures that moderately correlate with proficiency (r=.45–.64), or show an overall effect for proficiency for two or more proficiency levels (p<.05).

* Developmental measures that weakly correlate with proficiency (r=.25–.44), or show a trend towards an effect for proficiency (p<.10).

X Developmental measures that show no correlation with or effect for proficiency.

Error-free T-unit ratio (EFT/T)

EFT/T = total number of error-free T-units divided by total number of T-units

***	Hirano 91: analysis 2; Kawata 92; Tomita 90: analysis 1-level 1, level 2
**	Arnaud 92; Hirano 91: analysis 1; Larsen-Freeman 78; Larsen-Freeman & Strom 77; Tomita 90: analysis 1-level 3, analysis 2; Vann 79: analysis 1, analysis 2
*	Arthur 79: study 1; Casanave 94; Scott & Tucker 74
X	Arthur 79: study 2; Henry 96; Ishikawa 95: analysis 1–group 1, group 2; Larsen-Freeman 83: study 2–task 1, task 2, study 3; Tapia 93

The error-free T-unit ratio (EFT/T) was first used for the analysis of second language writing by Scott and Tucker (1974). Since then, twelve studies have found a significant relationship between error-free T-units per T-unit and proficiency, but eleven studies have not. Of the twelve significant studies, some investigated the relationship between error-free T-units per T-unit and program levels (Hirano, 1991: analysis 2; Larsen-Freeman, 1978; Larsen-Freeman & Strom, 1977), test scores (Arnaud, 1992; Hirano, 1991: analysis 1; Vann 1979: analysis 1) or grades (Kawata, 1992; Tomita, 1990: analysis 1-level 1, level 2, level 3), although four studies related to program or school level were not significant (Henry, 1996; Larsen-

Freeman, 1983: study 2–task 1, task 2; Tapia, 1993). In a discriminant analysis, Arthur (1979: study 2) didn't find a relationship between error-free T-units per T-unit and a rank ordering of compositions in an intact class.

Five longitudinal studies of change in intact classes were also not significant (Arthur, 1979: study 1; Ishikawa, 1995: analysis 1–group 1, group 2; Larsen-Freeman, 1983: study 3; Scott & Tucker, 1974), suggesting that error-free T-units per T-unit cannot capture short-term change within intact classes. Although the scores on the ratio of error-free T-units did increase over time in these longitudinal studies, there weren't significant differences. Casanave (1994) also found an overall increase in ratio of error-free T-units after three semesters of journal writing, but didn't test the differences statistically. However, in an analysis of individual learners' journal entries, she found that some learners vacillated in ratio of error-free T-units over time, although the time and topic conditions for writing journal entries can also be quite variable. This suggests that the reliability of measuring the ratio of error-free T-units across different writing samples from the same individual should be investigated further.

A comparison of the means across studies shows that there is a huge range from .133 to .852 error-free T-units per T-unit. This means that learners vary from as little as 1 out of 10 error-free T-units to almost nine out of ten, and certainly the actual ratio depends on how stringently error is defined, whether limited to only morphological and syntactic errors (Scott & Tucker, 1974) or including spelling and punctuation errors as well (Larsen-Freeman, 1978, 1983; Larsen-Freeman & Strom, 1977).

It should be noted that the error-free T-unit ratio measure (EFT/T) does not necessarily increase with proficiency. There was a lack of any relationship between the ratio of error-free T-units and program level for Larsen-Freeman (1983: study 2–task 1, task 2), who found that learners peaked in their error-free T-unit ratio at an intermediate level and then decreased at more advanced levels on both tasks. Tomita (1990: analysis 2) also found that scores on the error-free T-unit ratio increased from sophomore to junior level, but then decreased at the senior level. Henry (1996) found that scores on the error-free T-unit ratio increased from the first to second semesters of Russian study, but decreased at the fourth semester, then increased again at the sixth semester. There may not be a linear relationship between accuracy and proficiency in second language writing, with some advanced learners perhaps taking more risks and making more errors as a result (Tedick, 1990). Thus, it would be important to check how an increase in length of T-units (W/T) is related to a decrease in T-unit accuracy rate (EFT/T). In a discriminant analysis, Vann (1979) found that error-free T-units per T-unit (EFT/T) together with words per error-free T-unit (W/EFT), but not words per T-unit (W/T), accounted for the most variance in TOEFL scores, but we don't know how the measures were correlated with one another.

Error-free T-units per sentence (EFT/S)

EFT/S = total number of error-free T-units divided by total number of sentences

***	
**	Ho-Peng 83: task 1, task 2
*	
X	Ishikawa 95: analysis 1–group 1, group 2

The error-free T-units per sentence ratio (EFT/S) was first used by Ho-Peng (1983), with the sentence as the baseline production unit because it includes both coordination and subordination. This measure was not significant for Ishikawa's (1995: analysis 1) longitudinal study of two intact classes of beginning learners, although the scores on error-free T-units per sentence did increase with time. This measure was significant for Ho-Peng's (1983) study of two different writing tasks written by learners at three program levels, with the differences in the expected direction. A comparison of the means shows that there is a range from .19 to 1.14 error-free T-units per sentence. This means that learners vary from as little as one error-free T-unit per five sentences to one error-free T-unit per sentence.

Error-free T-units per word (EFT/W)

EFT/W = total number of error-free T-units divided by total number of words

***	
**	
*	
X	Nihalani 81

The error-free T-units per word ratio (EFT/W) was only used by Nihalani (1981), with word as the baseline production unit because it reflects an overall number of units that do not distinguish between sentence types. However, this measure was not significant for Nihalani (1981), who attempted to relate error-free T-units per word to grades assigned to writing samples collected from an advanced population of learners. Although the ratio of error-free T-units per word did increase as the grade increased, there was little difference between the A and B papers, and it is very likely that the final grade assignment depended on factors other than the number of error-free T-units. The compositions were a take-home assignment, which would also allow the writers the opportunity to correct their mistakes or obtain editing feedback. A potentially more useful word-based measure might be the number of error-free words per word (EFW/W), a measure that no one has used.

Error-free sentence ratio (EFS/S)

EFS/S = total number of error-free sentences divided by total number of sentences

***	
**	
*	
X	Tapia 93

The error-free sentence ratio (EFS/S) was used by Tapia (1993). Sentences were used as the baseline production unit rather than T-units because they reflect psychologically real production units for learners, and because they include both coordination and subordination (Bardovi-Harlig, 1992). However, this measure was not significant for Tapia's (1993) comparison of levels five and six out of a seven-level program, although there was an increase in score from level five to level six, with a range from .26 to .43 error-free sentences per sentence on various conditions. In holistic ratings of the writing samples, Tapia found no significant difference between the groups as well.

Error-free clause ratio (EFC/C)

EFC/C = total number of error-free clauses divided by total number of clauses

***	
**	Ishikawa 95: analysis 1–group 1
*	
X	Ishikawa 95: analysis 1–group 2; Tapia 93

The error-free clause ratio (EFC/C) was used by Tapia (1993) and Ishikawa (1995). Clauses were used as the baseline production unit rather than T-units because they are smaller production units for learners, so the domain for achieving 'error-free' status is smaller, and scores should be higher than on other error-free ratios (Ishikawa, 1995). However, this measure was significant only for one of Ishikawa's beginning-level groups over a three-month period (they improved from .30 to .45 error-free clauses per clause), although the other group also improved on this measure (from .33 to .40 error-free clauses per clause). Although Tapia (1993) found that level six of a seven-level program had higher scores (.67 and .70) than level five (.58 and .67), the results were not significant.

Error-free clauses per sentence (EFC/S)

EFC/S = total number of error-free clauses divided by total number of sentences

***	Ishikawa 95: analysis 2
**	Ishikawa 95: analysis 1–group 1, group 2
*	
X	

The error-free clauses per sentence ratio (EFC/S) was developed by Ishikawa (1995), with sentence as the baseline production unit because it includes both coordination and subordination. Although Ishikawa did not recognize it as the best measure in her study, a comparison of both her analyses suggests that error-free clauses per sentence was the best measure for capturing the growth in writing of these beginning-level writers over a three-month period. Both groups significantly improved on this measure (analysis 1), with Group 1 improving from .48 to .75 error-free clauses per sentence, and Group 2 improving from .47 to .70 error-free clauses per sentence. This measure also proved to be a highly reliable indicator of overall proficiency based on its high correlation with the summed z-scores on 24 measures for the pre-tests and post-tests of both groups (analysis 2). Presumably, this was because of an increase in the coordination of clauses along with an increase in the accuracy of those clauses.

Error-free clauses per T-unit (EFC/T)

EFC/T = total number of error-free clauses divided by total number of T-units

***	
**	Ishikawa 95: analysis 1–group 1
*	
X	Ishikawa 95: analysis 1–group 2

The error-free clauses per T-unit ratio (EFC/T) was developed by Ishikawa (1995), with T-unit as the baseline production unit. This measure was significant for only one of Ishikawa's (1995: analysis 1) two groups in her longitudinal study of beginning learners, although both groups improved (Group 1 from .49 to .72 error-free clauses per T-unit, and Group 2 from .49 to .62 error-free clauses per T-unit). T-unit may not be the best unit of analysis for beginning learners, because there are too many fragments not included in the analysis, as Ishikawa notes.

Words in error-free clauses ratio (WEFC/WC)

WEFC/WC = total number of words in error-free clauses divided by total number of words in clauses

***	
**	Ishikawa 95: analysis 1–group 1
*	
X	Ishikawa 95: analysis 1–group 2

This measure is somewhat unusual, because it is a variation on a measure that hasn't been used. That measure is the ratio of total number of words in error-free T-units to the total number of words in T-units (WEFT/WT), which would rise or fall primarily depending on how many error-free T-units there were, although it would be slightly dependent on how many average words per error-free T-unit there were as well. A more direct route to almost the same information would be to measure the ratio of error-free T-units to T-units (EFT/T) directly, with slight possible variation due to the degree of deviation from the average number of words per T-unit. But here, Ishikawa (1995) has developed a clause-based measure corresponding to WEFT/WT, which is the total number of words in error-free clauses divided by the total number of words in all clauses (WEFC/WC). The reason why the denominator is not total words is because some words occur in fragments that are contained in neither clauses or T-units. Her motivation was to examine error in the context of smaller units such as clauses, but she found a significant difference for only one of her groups over a three-month period (group 1 improved from .24 to .38 words in error-free clauses per total words in error-free clauses, and group 2 from .30 to .36). These results correspond to her results for error-free clauses per clause (EFC/C) and error-free clauses per T-unit (EFC/T), as expected.

Errors per T-unit (E/T)

E/T = total number of errors divided by total number of T-units

***	
**	Flahive & Snow 80: analysis 2-level 1, level 2, level 4, level 6; Perkins 80; Perkins & Leahy 80: analysis 1
*	Flahive & Snow 80: analysis 2-level 3, level 5
X	Flahive & Snow 80: analysis 1; Homburg 84: analysis 1; Perkins & Leahy 80: analysis 2

In four studies (11 analyses), researchers examined the number of errors per T-unit (E/T). For four of the levels that Flahive and Snow (1980: analysis 2) investigated, as well as Perkins (1980) and Perkins and Leahy (1980: analysis 1), there was a significant relationship between holistic ratings of essays and errors per T-unit. In all six cases, the essays were written by learners placed into the same level who were then differentiated by means of a holistic scale. For the other two levels investigated by Flahive and Snow (1980: analysis 2), there was a trend towards a relationship, but it wasn't significant. Of the studies that didn't find a significant relationship, one was a discriminant analysis of multiple proficiency levels (Flahive and Snow, 1980: analysis 1), one was a correlation between errors per T-unit and grades in a course (Perkins and Leahy, 1980: analysis 2), and one was a comparison between errors per T-unit and holistic ratings that differentiated placement level (Homburg, 1984: analysis 1). This means that the broad measure of errors per T-unit does not appear to discriminate among program or placement levels, but may relate to how teachers judge essays within a single level on the basis of a holistic scale. This measure is less an indication of development than it is an indication of what teachers are looking for when they make comparative judgments between learners at roughly the same level: overall accuracy. Of course, this type of generalization should be examined further in a variety of types of studies, but the results are certainly suggestive. The overall rates for errors per T-unit ranged from a .035 low for advanced learners (Perkins & Leahy, 1980) to a 1.51 high for students who failed a writing test (Perkins, 1980). The error rate for all six levels in Flahive & Snow (1980) ranged narrowly from 1.12 to 1.33 errors per T-unit, with no apparent connection to program level.

First-degree errors per T-unit (1DE/T)

1DE/T = total number of first-degree errors divided by total number of T-units (first-degree errors are completely understandable)

***	
**	
*	
X	Homburg 84: analysis 1

Homburg (1984: analysis 1) analyzed various types of errors based on their gravity, following Nas (1975). He looked at what he calls 'first-degree' errors, which include minor deviations in spelling, meaning, register, or grammatical form that do not interfere with understanding of the text at all. When he examined the ratio of first-degree errors to the total number of T-units (1DE/T), he found no significant effect, with .67 first-degree errors per T-unit for those who scored 5 out of 10 on a holistic scale, .58 for a score of 6, and .57 for a score of 7.

Second-degree errors per T-unit (2DE/T)

2DE/T = total number of second-degree errors divided by total number of T-units (second-degree errors are understandable only from context)

***	
**	Homburg 84: analysis 1
*	Homburg 84: analysis 2
X	

Homburg (1984) also examined what he calls 'second-degree' errors, which include serious deviations in spelling, meaning, grammatical form, or word order that are still interpretable within the context of the text, despite their seriousness. When he analyzed the ratio of second-degree errors to T-units (2DE/T), he found a significant difference between holistic ratings (analysis 1), and he found that it was a discriminant factor that correlated with holistic rating (analysis 2). The results are due to the marked difference for level seven, with both level five and six having .21 second-degree errors per T-unit, but level seven only .06. Furthermore, as Homburg recognizes, this classification is quite subjective; thus its utility as a developmental measure depends on whether there is interrater reliability in how error gravity is determined.

Third-degree errors per T-unit (3DE/T)

3DE/T = total number of third-degree errors divided by total number of T-units (third-degree errors completely interfere with understanding)

***	
**	
*	
X	Homburg 84: analysis 1

Homburg (1984: analysis 1) also examined what he calls 'third-degree' errors, which include serious deviations in form or meaning that completely interfere with the comprehensibility of the text. When he analyzed the ratio of third-degree errors to T-units (3DE/T), he found no significant difference between holistic ratings, because there were only .03 third-degree errors per T-unit for both level five and six, and .00 for level seven. These types of errors are so few that they are irrelevant in indicating level.

Errors per clause (E/C)

E/C = total number of errors divided by total number of clauses

***	Fischer 84: analysis 2
**	
*	Bardovi-Harlig & Bofman 89
X	Fischer 84: analysis 1

Fischer (1984) calculated the total number of errors per clause (E/C) in a study of the relationship between first-year French students written responses to a communicative situation and holistic scales that rated 'communicative pertinence' (analysis 1) and 'clarity' (analysis 2). Fischer found that errors per clause were not significantly correlated with communication ratings (r=−.019), but were strongly correlated with clarity ratings (r=.733). These results are consistent with the results for the errors per T-unit (E/T) measure discussed in the preceding section, with errors per clause and errors per T-unit both being clearly related to holistic judgments of error.

Bardovi-Harlig and Bofman (1989) calculated the total number of errors per clause (E/C) in their pass and non-pass groups of advanced learners, and reported that the non-pass group had .81 errors per clause, as opposed to .61 for the pass group. Although they did not report any statistical test of this difference, the results appear to be a trend in the anticipated direction. Bardovi-Harlig and Bofman (1989) used clauses rather than T-units as the basic measure of analysis because the T-unit includes one or more clauses, which "would build in an additional measure of complexity" (p. 32). Since the length of T-units varies a great deal depending on proficiency, Bardovi-Harlig and Bofman determined that it would be better to use the total number of clauses as the denominator. Bardovi-Harlig and Bofman (1989) also classified the errors as syntactic, morphological, or lexico-idiomatic, and calculated the number of errors per clause for each type, as reported in the next three sections.

Syntactic errors per clause (SynE/C)
SynE/C = total number of errors divided by total number of clauses

***	
**	
*	
X	Bardovi-Harlig & Bofman 89

Bardovi-Harlig and Bofman (1989) analyzed the number of syntactic errors per clause (SynE/C), which were errors in word order, embedding, complementation, coordination, fragments, or missing constituents. They found that syntactic errors per clause were the lowest of the three types of errors among their advanced learners of English (TOEFL: 543–567), and that there was no significant difference between the pass (.10) and non-pass (.14) groups with regard to ratio of syntactic errors per clause. This seems to indicate that the source of the pass versus non-pass decision was something other than the number of syntactic errors.

Morphological errors per clause (MorE/C)
MorE/C = total number of errors in morphology divided by total number of clauses

***	
**	
*	Bardovi-Harlig & Bofman 89
X	

Bardovi-Harlig and Bofman (1989) also analyzed the number of morphological errors per clause (MorE/C), which were errors in plural marking, subject-verb agreement, articles, determiners, prepositions, and derivational morphemes such as *-ment*. They found that the number of morphological errors per clause was the highest of the three types of errors among the advanced learners of English, and that there was a near-significant difference between the pass (.36) and non-pass (.49) groups with regard to morphological errors per clause. This seems to indicate that morphological errors persist at advanced levels and that morphological errors per clause may somewhat affect pass/fail decisions. However, since the context for this study is so limited (a pass/fail decision for advanced students), this measure needs to be investigated across program levels.

Lexical errors per clause (LexE/C)

LexE/C = total number of lexical errors divided by total number of clauses

***	
**	Bardovi-Harlig & Bofman 89
*	
X	

Bardovi-Harlig and Bofman (1989) also analyzed the number of lexical errors per clause (LexE/C), which were errors in lexical choice or idiomatic usage. They found that the number of lexical errors per clause was the second highest of the three types of errors among the advanced learners of English, and that there was a significant difference between the pass (.16) and non-pass (.25) groups with regard to lexical errors per clause. This seems to indicate that lexical errors persist at advanced levels, although less so than morphological errors, and that lexical errors are stronger determinants of pass-fail decisions than either morphological or syntactic errors, at least in this context. This measure also needs to be investigated across program levels.

Verb lexical errors per verb (VLexE/V)

VLexE/V = total number of verb lexical errors divided by total number of verbs

***	
**	Harley & King 89
*	
X	

In Harley & King's (1989) study of verb lexis in the compositions of French immersion students, they used a measure of verb lexical errors per verb (VLexE/V) to distinguish between 6th-grade level English-speaking learners of French and their native-speaking counterparts. They defined lexical errors as malformations of verb stems, the use of native language verb stems, or incorrect use in the context, but not as errors of tense or agreement. Although they did find that lexical error rate significantly distinguished between their two groups (the second language group with .06 verb lexical errors but the native language group with .01 verb lexical errors), it doesn't mean that this is a good measure of second language writing development, since it was a comparison between second language and native speakers. Further studies with learners at different proficiency levels would be needed to determine the relevance to writing development.

Lexical errors per lexical word (LexE/LW)

LexE/LW = total number of lexical errors divided by total number of lexical words

***	
**	
*	Engber 95
X	

Engber (1995) developed a lexical error ratio, in which she calculated the number of lexical errors per lexical word (LexE/LW). She counted errors of incorrect word choice, collocation, and derivation, but disregarded errors of verbal morphology. When she compared lexical errors per lexical word to holistic ratings, she found a trend towards significance. Zughoul (1991) identified 13 different lexical error types in second language writing (assumed synonyms, literal translation from the native language, similar forms, circumlocution, etc.), but did not analyze the relationship between these errors and proficiency.

Errors per word (E/W)

E/W = total number of errors divided by total number of words

***	Linnarud 86: analysis 2
**	Hyltenstam 92
*	
X	

Linnarud (1986: analysis 2) used an errors per word ratio (E/W) to examine the relationship between errors and holistic ratings of second language writers' picture descriptions, and found a significant and strong correlation. Hyltenstam (1992) found a significant difference between second language and native learners on the same measure. Although Hyltenstam collapsed written and oral data together for the statistical test of overall error rate, he provides separate means for errors per word by modality. In Hyltenstam's study, the ratios of errors per word are very low (these were advanced groups of learners), ranging from .2 to 1.3 errors per 100 words depending on the group and modality.

Grammatical errors per word (GrE/W)
GrE/W = total number of grammatical errors divided by total number of words

***	
**	Arnaud 92; Arthur 79: study 2
*	Scott & Tucker 74
X	Arthur 79: study 1

Various researchers have analyzed the number of grammatical errors per word (GrE/W) in essays, although with mixed results. Arnaud (1992) found that grammatical errors per word correlated with test scores, and Arthur (1979) found that grammatical errors per word was a discriminant factor in accounting for the variance of holistic rankings, but didn't correlate with classroom gains over time. Scott and Tucker (1974) did not do any statistical analysis of the relationship between grammatical errors and increases in proficiency attained at the end of a course, although it appears that there was a developmental trend in the right direction for the number of overall errors. In longitudinal studies of intact classes, Arnaud (1992) found that the grammatical errors per 100 words decreased from 2.43 to 1.75 for advanced learners, Arthur (1979) found that they decreased from 17.35 to 16.77 for low-intermediate learners, and Scott and Tucker (1974) found that they decreased from 8.72 to 6.03 for low-intermediate learners.

Arthur (1979) did not define "grammatical" error in his study, although he did contrast errors of subject-verb agreement, adverb placement, and gerund/infinitive use with semantic errors. Arnaud (1992) included errors on closed-class members but not irregular verb forms in his definition of grammatical errors, because he considered the latter errors to be lexical. Scott & Tucker (1974) classified a whole range of errors and the percentages at which they occurred, but did not analyze them statistically. Since Bardovi-Harlig & Bofman (1989) found that morphological errors were far more prevalent than syntactic errors at advanced levels, analyzing these errors separately might discriminate among proficiency levels better.

Semantic errors per error (SemE/E)
SemE/E = Total number of semantic errors divided by total number of errors

***	
**	
*	
X	Arthur 79: study 1, study 2

Arthur (1979) defines semantic errors as those that "distort meaning". However, considering that he provides as examples of semantic errors the use of the present tense to refer to past events, or the use of "killed" for "died," it appears that his semantic errors included grammatical and lexical errors as well. When he examined the longitudinal progression of a low-intermediate class of students on the ratio of semantic errors to total errors (study 1), as well as correlations between a holistic rank ordering and semantic errors per total errors (study 2), he found no significant relationship. In the longitudinal study, he found a decrease from 36.24 to 34.63 semantic errors per 100 errors from the first half of the class to the second half. Perhaps a greater decrease would have been noted if only the first and last compositions had been compared.

Correct connectors per word (CorrCN/W)
CorrCN/W = total number of connectors used correctly divided by total number of words

***	
**	
*	
X	Evola et al. 80: analysis 2

Evola et al. (1980: analysis 2) analyzed the relationship between holistic ratings of writing samples written by learners in five program levels and the ratio of correct connectors to total number of words (CorrCN/W), finding no significant relationship. They did not report the means for this measure.

Correct pronouns per word (CorrPN/W)
CorrPN/W = total number of pronouns used correctly divided by total number of words

***	
**	
*	
X	Evola et al. 80: analysis 2

Evola et al. (1980: analysis 2) also analyzed the relationship between holistic ratings of writing samples written by learners in five program levels and the ratio of correct pronouns to total number of words (CorrPN/W), finding no significant relationship. They did not report the means for this measure.

Correct article ratio (CorrART/CX)
CorrART/CX = total number of articles used correctly divided by total number of contexts either required or supplied

***	
**	Cumming & Mellow 96: analysis 1, analysis 2
*	
X	Evola et al. 80: analysis 2

Both Evola et al. (1980: analysis 2) and Cumming and Mellow (1996: analysis 1, analysis 2) calculated the number of articles used correctly in contexts where the article was either required or supplied (CorrART/CX). While Evola et al. found no significant relationship between correct article use and holistic ratings of writing samples written by learners in five program levels, Cumming and Mellow did find a significant relationship between correct article use and intermediate versus advanced placement judgments for French learners of English (74.8 versus 86.8 correct articles per context), and intermediate versus advanced TOEFL scores for Japanese learners of English (67.6 versus 77.8 correct articles per context). However, it is unclear whether correct article use can differentiate more fine-tuned proficiency levels. Cumming and Mellow suggested that accuracy of article use may be an indicator of second language development that is unrelated to writing expertise.

Correct definite article ratio (CorrDEF/CX)

CorrDEF/CX = total number of definite articles used correctly divided by total number of contexts either required or supplied

***	
**	Cumming & Mellow 96: analysis 2
*	
X	Cumming & Mellow 96: analysis 1

Cumming and Mellow (1996) also examined more specific distinctions in the correct use of articles, separating the use of definite articles from indefinite articles. When they analyzed the number of correct definite articles used in either required or supplied contexts (CorrDEF/CX), they found that this measure only significantly related to the Japanese learners of English, who were differentiated into an intermediate group (407–470) and advanced group (473–577) by TOEFL score. These two Japanese groups had 62.5 versus 77.8 correct definite articles per context; whereas the two French intermediate and advanced groups had 76.9 versus 85.8 correct definite articles per context.

Correct indefinite article ratio (CorrINDEF/CX)

CorrINDEF/CX = total number of indefinite articles used correctly divided by total number of contexts either required or supplied

***	
**	Cumming & Mellow 96: analysis 1
*	
X	Cumming & Mellow 96: analysis 2

When Cumming and Mellow (1996) analyzed the number of correct indefinite articles used in either required or supplied contexts (CorrINDEF/CX), they found that this measure only significantly related to the French learners of English, who were differentiated into an intermediate group and advanced group on the basis of variables such as program placement and length of exposure. These two French groups had 77.3 versus 89.8 correct indefinite articles per context; whereas the two Japanese intermediate and advanced groups had 74.2 versus 79.6 correct indefinite articles per context.

Correct plural ratio (CorrPL/CX)
CorrPL/CX = total number of plurals used correctly divided by total number of contexts either required or supplied

***	
**	
*	
X	Cumming & Mellow 96: analysis 1, analysis 2

Cumming & Mellow (1996) also calculated the proportion of correctly used plurals in either required or supplied contexts (CorrPL/CX), but found no correlation between accuracy on this measure and level of proficiency for either French learners or Japanese learners of English. The accuracy scores varied from 65.1 to 79.0 correct plurals per context. They also looked at correct suppliance of third-person singular, but found so few relevant cases that they could not perform a statistical analysis.

ACCURACY INDICES

Most of the accuracy indices proposed by researchers to measure development appear to significantly relate to second language proficiency, as shown in Table 6 below. Indices that count all types of errors correlate with holistic ratings by teachers (Kaczmarek, 1980) and with length of school exposure to the second language for children (Gipps & Ewen, 1974). Accuracy indices that focus on lexical errors correlate with a discrete point vocabulary test (Arnaud, 1992) and with holistic ratings of samples (Engber, 1995). However, accuracy indices that focus on a single type of grammatical error are unable to discriminate among holistic ratings of samples (Evola et al., 1980).

Table 6. Accuracy indices: Number of studies by type of result

measure	code	***	**	*	X
intelligibility index	IntellIndex		1		
error index	Error Index	2			
error formula 1	EF1				2
error formula 2	EF2			1	
lexical quality index	LexQualIndex		1		
lexical accuracy index	LexAccIndex		1		

*** Developmental measures that highly correlate with proficiency (r=.65+), or show an overall effect for proficiency (p<.05) together with a significant difference between three or more adjacent proficiency levels (p<.05).

** Developmental measures that moderately correlate with proficiency (r=.45–.64), or show an overall effect for proficiency for two or more proficiency levels (p<.05).

* Developmental measures that weakly correlate with proficiency (r=.25–.44), or show a trend towards an effect for proficiency (p<.10).

X Developmental measures that show no correlation with or effect for proficiency.

Intelligibility index (IntellIndex)
IntellIndex = sum of points for the intelligibility of each T-unit:
    0=unintelligible;
    1=partly intelligible;
    2=completely intelligible;
    3=completely accurate

***	
**	Gipps & Ewen 74
*	
X	

Gipps and Ewen (1974) applied a scale of intelligibility to each T-unit identified in children's second language writing. The T-unit was rated a 0 if it was completely unintelligible, a 1 if it was partly intelligible, a 2 if it was completely intelligible, and a 3 if it was completely accurate. The final score was the sum of all the T-unit scores. They found a high interrater reliability on the classification of the T-units (.98), and a significant difference in the intelligibility index score between three groups of children that differed on how long the children had been using the second language in school (ignoring age differences).

Error index (ErrorIndex)

ErrorIndex = number of error-free words minus number of errors divided by number of error-free words

***	Kaczmarek 80: scale 1, scale 2
**	
*	
X	

Kaczmarek (1980) created an error index that she compared to two holistic rating scales (ability, comprehensibility) that were applied to the compositions of university-level students enrolled in an ESL program. She began by having raters rewrite a student's composition following the text closely, and then count the error-free words in the subject's original rendition as well as the number of errors, which included words that were not necessary, missing words, and non-idiomatic sequences. The error index was calculated by subtracting the number of errors from the error-free words, and dividing by the total number of error-free words (EFW-E/EFW). She found a high correlation between the error index and two holistic scales used to rate the compositions, confirming once again that composition raters pay attention to the errors found in second language learners' writing.

Error formula 1 (EF1)

EF1 = number of correct usages minus number of errors divided by number of words (applied to conjunctions and pronouns)

***	
**	
*	
X	Evola et al. 80: analysis 2 — conjunctions, pronouns

Evola et al. (1980) created an error formula (EF1) that could be used to analyze the correctness of particular grammatical morphemes, such as conjunctions or pronouns. The formula calculates the number of correct usages minus the number of errors divided by the number of words produced. Uses of conjunctions counted as errors if they "did not convey an appropriate relationship between two phrases or clauses" (p. 179), and uses of pronouns were counted as errors if they did not refer to an identifiable referent, or if they were incorrectly formed in person, number, gender, or case. They found that there was no significant relationship between the error formula and holistic ratings on the compositions written by learners at a wide range of proficiency levels. That is probably because the measures are so finely-tuned, whereas a holistic scale is just that: holistic. No one type of error is going to single-handedly determine a holistic rating.

Error formula 2 (EF2)
EF2 = number of correct uses minus number of errors divided by number of obligatory contexts (applied to articles)

***	
**	
*	Evola et al. 80: analysis 2 — articles
X	

Evola et al. (1980) created another error formula in order to analyze the use of articles in second language compositions. This formula (EF2) calculates the number of correct uses in obligatory contexts minus the number of errors divided by the total number of obligatory contexts. Uses of articles counted as whole errors if they did not appear where they were required by the context, or if they appeared where they were not required. They were counted as half errors if the wrong article appeared in an obligatory context for an article. They found that there was no significant relationship between the error formula and holistic ratings on the compositions written by learners at a wide range of proficiency levels, although there was a weak correlation. Again, that is probably because no one type of error is going to single-handedly determine a holistic rating.

Lexical quality index (LexQualIndex)
LexQualIndex = total number of lexical word types plus total number of rare word types minus two times the number of erroneous tokens

***	
**	Arnaud 92
*	
X	

Arnaud (1992) chose to use a lexical quality formula because other lexical ratio measures yielded low or non-significant correlations with discrete-item tests. He controlled the text length of writing samples by using the shortest texts as length limits in a set of two timed writings (208 and 241 words). Lexical quality was determined by a formula that calculated the total number of lexical word types plus the total number of rare word types minus two times the number of erroneous lexical words on same length samples (LWT+RWT–2LWE). This measure combines lexical variation and lexical accuracy in one measure. Arnaud determined that rare word types were words that do not occur in the syllabus during the first four years of secondary education in France. He counted words as errors if they were semantically wrong, part of a bad collocation, contained a derivational error, or were misspelled. He did not count errors on closed-class words except for prepositions that were specified by the verb (e.g., interested in). He found that there was a significant correlation between the lexical quality formula and scores on a discrete item vocabulary test. It is not clear how this measure would relate to more global measures of proficiency level.

Lexical accuracy index (LexAccIndex)
LexAccIndex = total number of lexical word types minus total number of lexical errors divided by total number of lexical words

***	
**	Engber 95
*	
X	

Engber (1995) proposed a type of lexical variation measure that is also a lexical accuracy index because it is a formula that captures the relationship between lexical errors and lexical word types. This measure combines lexical variation and lexical accuracy in one measure. The lexical accuracy index calculates the number of lexical word types minus the number of lexical errors divided by the number of lexical words (LWT-LE/LW). Lexical errors include errors of lexical choice, collocation, derivational morphology, and spelling. This formula captures the intuition that writers with higher language proficiency will produce more lexical variation with fewer lexical errors, resulting in a higher score. Engber found that this measure was significantly related to holistic ratings of the writing samples of Farsi and Arabic writers distributed across five program levels.

CONCLUSION: ACCURACY MEASURES

None of the frequently-used accuracy measures are clearly related to program or school level, but do appear to be related to holistic ratings and short-term change in intact classes. These measures are the number of error-free T-units (EFT), error-free T-units per T-unit (EFT/T), and errors per T-unit (E/T). For studies that used program or school levels as the measure of proficiency, some found a linear relationship to these developmental measures, while others did not, as Table 7 shows. The EFT and EFT/T measures should increase with proficiency, while the E/T measures should decline with proficiency; inconsistent results appear in shaded cells.

Table 7: Comparison of means on accuracy measures across studies that examine multiple programs or school levels

Timed essay, proficiency = program or school level			
study/levels	EFT	EFT/T	E/T
Flahive & Snow, 1980			
level 1			1.26
level 2			1.12
level 3			1.28
level 4			1.26
level 5			1.21
level 6			1.33
Henry, 1996			
semester 1		.32	
semester 2		.34	
semester 4		.26	
semester 6		.36	
Hirano, 1991			
low	2.10	.15	
mid	3.88	.23	
high	5.06	.33	
Larsen-Freeman, 1978			
level 1		.11	
level 2		.19	
level 3		.22	
level 4		.34	
level 5		.50	
Larsen-Freeman, 1983			
level 2		.42	
level 3		.43	
level 4		.38	
Tapia, 1993			
level 5		.34	
level 6		.43	

continued…

Table 7: Comparison of means on accuracy measures across studies that examine multiple programs or school levels (cont.)

Timed essay, proficiency = program or school level			
study/levels	EFT	EFT/T	E/T
Tedick, 1990			
beginning	4.86		
intermediate	7.42		
advanced	8.89		
Tomita, 1990			
grade 10	5.35	.38	
grade 11	6.68	.45	
grade 12	5.32	.39	

Rewriting task, proficiency = program or school level			
study/levels	EFT	EFT/T	E/T
Larsen-Freeman, 1983			
level 1		.74	
level 2		.85	
level 3		.78	
level 4		.76	
Sharma, 1980			
low intermediate	6.15		
high intermediate	5.30		
advanced	8.95		

Note: Shaded cells indicate results inconsistent with the theory that EFT and EFT/T measures should increase with proficiency, while the E/T measures should decline.

Here, six out of ten studies do not show a linear progression of increasing accuracy based on program or school level, which is quite a different result than what we found for the fluency measures in the preceding chapter.

However, in studies that used holistic ratings across multiple proficiency levels or holistic ratings within intact classes or for learners with the same narrow range of test scores, there does appear to be a linear relationship between these three measures (EFT, EFT/T, E/T) and ratings, as Table 8 shows. One study that used a fourth measure, errors per clause (E/C), suggests that this measure may also be important to consider.

Table 8: Comparison of means on accuracy measures across studies that examine holistic rating scales of learners at multiple or similar levels

| Timed essay, proficiency = holistic rating of multiple levels | | | | |
study/levels	EFT	EFT/T	E/T	E/C
Homburg, 1984				
rating 5	5.40		.91	
rating 6	8.60		.83	
rating 7	10.00		.74	
Larsen-Freeman & Strom, 1977				
'poor'		3.5		
'fair'		11.7		
'average'		17.2		
'good'		25.5		
'excellent'		28.5		

| Timed essay, proficiency = holistic rating of intact class or learners at same test level | | | | |
study/levels	EFT	EFT/T	E/T	E/C
Bardovi-Harlig & Bofman, 1989				
'non-pass'				.81
'pass'				.61
Perkins, 1980				
'fail'	3.87		1.51	
'pass minus'	7.33		1.10	
'pass'	10.73		.70	

| Timed essay, proficiency = holistic rating of intact class or learners at same test level | | | | |
study/levels	EFT	EFT/T	E/T	E/C
Perkins & Leahy, 1980				
L2 freshmen	15.00		.67	
NS freshmen	28.13		.30	

Finally, in studies where proficiency was defined as short-term change within an intact class, not only are these three measures (EFT, EFT/T, E/T) consistently linear in progression, but Ishikawa's (1995) study of two intact classes also suggests that three clause-based error measures, error-free clauses (EFC), error-free clauses per clause (EFC/C), and error-free clauses per sentence (EFC/S), may be important measures of accuracy, as Table 9 shows.

Table 9: Comparison of means on accuracy measures across studies that examine longitudinal change

| study/levels | Proficiency = short-term change in intact class | | | | |
	EFC	EFT	EFT/T	EFC/C	EFC/S
Arthur, 1979					
first half		25.21			
second half		28.89			
Ishikawa, 1995; Group 1					
pre	5.31	2.31	.20	.30	.48
post	9.38	4.03	.29	.45	.75
Ishikawa, 1995; Group 2					
pre	5.93	3.32	.25	.33	.47
post	8.36	4.54	.31	.40	.70
Larsen-Freeman, 1983					
time 1			.597		
time 5			.607		
Scott & Tucker, 1974					
time 1			.494		
time 2			.539		

These complex results for accuracy measures are difficult to interpret because they differ based on how proficiency level is determined. Perhaps measures of error may be related to teachers' judgments and to short-term changes related to instruction, but may only be indirectly related to widely-spaced program levels. Perhaps error measures are not related to 'development' as a construct but rather to 'error' as a construct, and these two may be different but indirectly-related factors in language growth.

In a particularly revealing study of error, Bardovi-Harlig and Bofman (1989) found that both a pass and non-pass group of advanced learners showed the same proportion of type of errors — about .57 morphological errors, .27 lexical-idiomatic, and .15 syntactic, even though the non-pass group had more errors overall. They concluded that syntactic features of language are the least difficult to acquire while morphological features are the most difficult to acquire. Larsen-Freeman (1983) also pointed out that the majority of errors were morphological, and included articles, prepositions, and verb tense. Cumming and Mellow (1996) go further in identifying developmental stages in morphology from plural marking to definite then indefinite articles to subject-verb agreement.

As Bardovi-Harlig and Bofman (1989) pointed out, there may be a difference between the more universal, core, global, and resilient syntactic features of language, which are acquired earlier and are not as sensitive to variation in input, and the more language-specific, peripheral, local, and fragile morphological features of language. Bardovi-Harlig and Bofman (1989) call this a "strong syntax-weak morphology stage" (p. 28). However, this does not explain why lexical errors are somewhat intermediate, unless they represent the interface between syntax and morphology. The discovery of how errors relate to development, and why measures of error seem to be different than measures of fluency or complexity in how they relate to proficiency measures, are both important areas for future research.

CHAPTER FOUR

THE GRAMMATICAL COMPLEXITY MEASURES

Grammatical complexity is manifest in writing primarily in terms of grammatical variation and sophistication. Foster and Skehan (1996, p. 303) defined development in grammatical complexity as "progressively more elaborate language" and "a greater variety of syntactic patterning." Grammatical complexity means that a wide variety of both basic and sophisticated structures are available and can be accessed quickly, whereas a lack of complexity means that only a narrow range of basic structures are available or can be accessed. An analysis of grammatical complexity is not concerned with how many production units are present in the writing (such as clauses, T-units, or sentences), but with how varied or sophisticated the production units are. Learners who have more grammatical structures available to them are able to vary their structural choices in written production.

Restructuring may be the learning process which causes growth in grammatical complexity, through "the evolution of increasingly abstract representations of knowledge" (Foster & Skehan, 1996; Schmidt, 1992, p. 369). Schmidt (1992) considered restructuring to be something quite different from automaticity, but if automaticity is viewed as the strengthening of memories for chunks, with chunk sequences being related to one another in increasingly complex patterns, then restructuring may be a natural outcome of automaticity. McLaughlin (1983) claimed that automaticity at lower levels of processing frees up resources for restructuring at higher levels, and Ellis (1996) claimed that memory for chunks is the basis of not only automaticity, but also higher-level restructuring. Perhaps learning begins with an exposure to instances; increasing exposure to and memory for instances causes generalizations to form, which can then be overwhelmed by further exposure to instances that are exceptions. Gradually, a more complex representation that accounts for many instances (both regular and irregular) develops, while at the same time access becomes increasingly automatic.

The production units used to measure growth in grammatical complexity are clauses, T-units, and sentences. Grammatical complexity measures are of two types: those that analyze the clauses, sentences, or T-units in terms of each other (e.g., clauses per sentence, dependent clauses per T-unit, T-units per sentence); and those that analyze the presence of specific grammatical structures in relation to clauses, T-units, or sentences (e.g., passives per sentence, nominals per T-unit). These production units have been defined in various ways in the calculation of grammatical complexity measures (Polio, 1997), and sometimes the definitions conflict:

Clause = a phrase dominated by VP or S (Bardovi-Harlig & Bofman, 1989) or

a structure with a subject and a finite verb (Hunt, 1965; Polio, 1997)

With respect to sentence fragments

- a clause can include sentence fragments with no overt verb (Bardovi-Harlig & Bofman, 1989)
- a clause does not include fragments unless they are a complete thought (Ishikawa, 1995)

T-unit = a main clause plus any subordinate clauses (Hunt, 1965):

With respect to sentence fragments

- a T-unit can include sentence fragments punctuated by the writer (Bardovi- Harlig & Bofman, 1989; Tapia, 1993)
- a T-unit does not include sentence fragments (Ishikawa, 1995; Hirano, 1991; Vann, 1979)

With respect to punctuation

- a T-unit can occur across sentences punctuated by the writer (Hunt, 1965)
- a T-unit can occur only within sentences punctuated by the writer (Homburg, 1984; Ishikawa, 1995)

Sentence = group of words punctuated by the writer (Hunt, 1965; Tapia, 1993)

Hunt (1965) first developed the T-unit as a measure of children's syntactic maturity in writing, defining the T-unit as a 'minimal terminable unit' consisting of a main (i.e. independent) clause plus any subordinate clauses. The children in Hunt's study used coordinated, run-on sentences in their writing at earlier ages, which gradually decreased as they began to use more sophisticated types of subordination, embedding, and modification. It should be remembered that Hunt tested the usefulness of the T-unit for widely-spaced school levels (the 4th, 8th, and 12th grades). The T-unit has also been widely used in second language studies of writing, the goal being to indicate second language learners' "ability to exploit the embedding processes available in the target language" (Sharma, 1980, p. 320).

The T-unit has been criticized because it contains subordination but not coordination as part of its definition, thus obscuring inappropriate coordinations by separating them into different T-units (Bardovi-Harlig, 1992). As a result, Bardovi-Harlig argues for the sentence as a more psychologically and pedagogically real production unit for adult second language learners. However, Ishikawa (1995) argues that the clause may be a better production unit for tapping into beginning level writing because it is smaller than a T-unit, thus providing a smaller context for examining language growth in a variety of ways.

Although the T-unit appears to be a measure that is defined by subordination, it can also be thought of as nothing more than a representation of the independent clauses in a piece of writing, since each T-unit consists of one independent clause (Hunt, 1965). Whether it is more desirable to use the number of independent clauses (T-units) or the number of clauses as a basis of comparison to other structures present in the writing depends on the purpose. For example, it may not be appropriate to count the number of complex nominals per T-unit (as in Cooper, 1976). Since complex nominals occur in all clause types, not just independent clauses, it would be more appropriate to count the number of complex nominals per clause, which would be neutral with respect to clause type.

One crucial and unresolved issue in an examination of grammatical complexity measures is how clause types are defined by researchers. There are four types of finite clauses that occur in writing: independent clauses (i.e. main clauses), adverbial clauses, adjective clauses (i.e. relative clauses), and nominal clauses (i.e. noun clauses, including both that-clauses and interrogative clauses). Hunt (1965) defined T-units as main clauses plus any subordinate clauses, with subordinate clauses including all adverbial, adjective, and nominal clauses. This has led researchers such as Bardovi-Harlig and Bofman (1989, p. 20) to define a complex sentence as "a multiclausal sentence exhibiting subordination."

Adjective and nominal clauses are always embedded within independent or adverbial clauses, with adjective clauses acting as modifiers of head nouns, and nominal clauses acting as noun phrases. In contrast, adverbial clauses are always appended to independent clauses on either end, as the following examples show:

Independent/main clause

He is *heroic* because he saved a child's life.

Adverbial/subordinate clause

Because he saved a child's life, he is heroic.

Adjective/relative clause

He, *who has never been brave*, is heroic because he saved a child *who was drowning*.

Nominal/noun clause

What he has done is heroic because he saved a child from *what would have been certain death*.

Furthermore, adverbial, adjective, and nominal clauses can all be reduced to adjective, prepositional, participial, gerund, or infinitive phrases, which are the phrasal means by which sentence complexity can be achieved. The use of phrases rather than clauses will have the effect of reducing the number of words per T-unit, as the following comparisons show:

Adverbial clause reduced to a participle:

Because he saved a child's life, he is heroic.

Having saved a child's life, he is heroic.

Adjective clause reduced to a prepositional phrase or adjective:

He, *who is at heart a timid soul*, is heroic because he saved a child *who was drowning.*

He, *at heart a timid soul*, is heroic because he saved a *drowning* child.

Nominal clause reduced to a gerund or infinitive:

That he saved a child is all the more heroic because he is so timid.

Saving a child is all the more heroic because he is so timid.

To save a child is all the more heroic when someone is so timid.

One question is whether either of these versions can be considered more grammatically complex than the other. We think that it is impossible to defend a choice in strictly grammatical terms, but on the basis of usage, more advanced writers may tend to use the more reduced forms (Cooper, 1976; Hunt, 1965; Monroe, 1975; Sharma, 1980).

Reductions from clauses to phrases can affect the clause count as well, depending on how clause is defined. In Hunt's (1965) definition, clauses must have subjects and a finite verb, which means that only independent, adverbial, adjective, and nominal clauses count as clauses. Hunt dismisses the definition of LaBrant (1934), who counted all predicates as clauses, treating coordinated verbs as separate clauses. The latter approach is similar to Bardovi-Harlig and Bofman (1989), who considered clauses to be phrases that are dominated by a VP or an S. This means that subjects can be omitted or that verbs can be coordinated. Bardovi-Harlig and Bofman also included non-finite verb phrases (i.e., adverbial participle phrases and nominal gerund or infinitive phrases) in their definition of clause (personal communication). The difference between these two methods of counting clauses (finite VPs with subjects versus all VPs) could lead to differences in other measures that use the number of clauses as a base measure.

The existence of four finite clause types has led some researchers to define groups of clauses in different ways. Some have made a distinction between independent clauses and dependent, secondary, or subordinate clauses, including all adverbial, adjective, and nominal clauses in the definition of dependent (Cooper, 1976), secondary (Kameen, 1979), or subordinate (Hunt, 1965; Monroe, 1976). Others have treated subordinate clauses as being limited to adverbial clauses alone. For example, Homburg (1984) contrasted independent and dependent clauses, but defined dependent clauses as subordinate clauses and relative clauses, excluding nominal clauses (which are embedded but not dependent). Other researchers have made a three-way distinction between independent clauses, subordinate clauses, and embedded clauses, defining embedded clauses as adjective and nominal clauses (Tapia, 1993).

This is quite tricky, actually, because adverbial and adjective clauses are both dependent while nominal clauses are not, but adjective and nominal clauses are both embedded, while adverbial clauses are not. We think it's important not to collapse the four finite clause types into larger subcategories, but to keep each type distinct. For example, Hunt (1965) found that adverbial clauses did not increase significantly with language development, while nominal clauses and adjective clauses did. Increases in adjective clauses showed the strongest relationship to age of the writer, as well as the strongest correlation with increases in words per T-unit (W/T).

There have been a number of proposals about how grammatical complexity in written language develops, beginning with the claim that writers move from coordination to subordination to reduced phrases (Hunt, 1965). That proposal has been filled out somewhat for adult second language learners, with Ishikawa (1995) suggesting that at the very beginning stages, writers move from fragments to clauses to T-units, and Monroe (1975), Cooper (1976) and Sharma (1980) suggesting that writers move from coordination to subordination to the reduction of clauses to phrases. Furthermore, Sharma (1980) suggests that although there is a stage when relative clauses increase, at the more advanced reduction stage they may decrease in favor of adjectives and prepositional phrases. Hunt (1965) also pointed out that the number of infinitive and participle modifiers of nouns, the number of 'near-clause' nominals (infinitives and gerunds), and the number of nominalizations all increase at later stages of language development. An extrapolation from these discussions suggests that the stages may proceed (roughly) as follows:

fragments

main clauses

coordinate clauses

adverbial clauses

adjective and nominal clauses

adjectival, adverbial, and nominal verb phrases

Certainly these proposed 'stages' would overlap in any actual writing sample; these types of proposals suggest only that there would be emergence of a certain type of structure at the expense of other structures at a certain stage of development. Perhaps every one of these structural stages develops non-linearly, with a steady increase as learners approach a particular stage, followed by a decline as they leave it (following the shape of an omega Ω symbol, and similar to the concept of 'flooding' proposed by Huebner, 1983). Notice that this is the inverse pattern of the famous U of developmental fame. A U-shaped developmental pattern suggests an initial stage of accuracy, followed by a decrease in accuracy, followed by an increase in accuracy.[1] Perhaps the accuracy U corresponds to a complexity Ω: as the structure grows in use, it becomes less accurate; as the use of the structure moderates, it becomes more accurate. However, in the previous section we also discussed a potential accuracy N shape (a zigzag) to represent how error-free T-units per T-unit (EFT/T) may change in relationship to language development (from an early inaccurate stage followed by a more accurate one, followed by a decline and then an increase again). Of course, error-free T-units are more global in scope than the individual phenomena that gave rise to the U shape, so the patterns may be different.

Of course, this is completely speculative, and clearly direct investigation is needed in a comparison of potential accuracy and complexity trade-offs. Perhaps we would find out more about development at all stages if we adequately measured all clause types and whether or not the types were error-free, leading to such measures as the number of adjective clauses per clause (AdjC/C) along with the number of error-free adjective clauses per clause (EFAdjC/C). The current batch of accuracy and complexity measures, when viewed as a whole, seem like nothing more than hopeful, uncoordinated stabs in the dark that hint at something but reveal very little as yet.

Although there has been a great deal of focus on clause-related measures as indicators of grammatical complexity in writing, there has been some recognition that language development includes other structures as well. The only tense/aspect structure that has been investigated is the use of passives (Kameen, 1979), while others have examined cohesive devices such as connectors, pronouns, and articles (Homburg, 1984; Evola et al., 1980). There has also been a search for an index of complexity that would encompass a wide range of grammatical structures. Both Flahive and Snow (1980) and Perkins (1980) assigned weights to certain morphological and syntactic structures based on theoretical assumptions about their complexity, developing formulas to weigh the degree of complexity present in the writing. While Perkins calculated his complexity score on the basis of sentences, Flahive and Snow calculated their complexity score on the basis of T-units. In our view, the goal of these grammatical complexity studies should be to correlate individual measures for a wide variety of structures. For instance, one goal could be to find a relationship between tense, article, and clause development, but that is largely uncharted territory.

---

[1] However, it is important to realize that the accuracy of the initial point on the accuracy U is a pretense — what appears to be accuracy is achieved because irregular items are initially learned as individual words. When broader generalizations about both regular and irregular items are learned, errors appear. What appears to be accuracy initially is not based on an accurate representation of the underlying system.

GRAMMATICAL COMPLEXITY FREQUENCIES

In general, the validity of frequency measures of grammatical complexity is doubtful because of the lack of a fixed delimiter as found in ratio measures. However, some researchers have counted the frequency of various complex structures that occur in second language writing if they imposed either a time limit on the writing (Evola et al., 1980; Homburg, 1984; Kameen, 1979; Kawata, 1992), or a conceptual limit in the form of a rewriting task, in which a simplified passage is provided that the learners rewrite using more complex constructions (Monroe, 1975; Sharma, 1980). Of these studies (see Table 10 below), the most noteworthy significant results were for reduced or dependent clauses (Homburg, 1984; Monroe, 1975), as well as passives (Kameen, 1979). An interesting proposal discussed by Cooper (1976), Monroe (1975), and Sharma (1980) is that reduced clauses are a measure of a late stage where more information is packed into a clause, thus reducing the number of clauses. Counting other types of clauses, such as adverbial, adjective, nominal, or relative clauses, did not significantly relate to proficiency levels. Nor did counting structures like prepositional phrases, preposed adjectives, or types of connectors. The only exception was Evola's (1980) study, in which they counted the number of pronouns, articles, and connectors, and found a significant relationship to five program levels, but not between adjacent levels.

Table 10. Grammatical complexity frequencies:
Number of studies by type of result

measure	code	***	**	*	X
reduced clauses	RedC	1			
dependent clauses	DepC		1	1	1
passives	Pass		1		
passive sentences	PassS		2		
adverbial clauses	AdvC				1
adjective clauses	AdjC				2
nominal clauses	NomC				1
prepositional phrases	PP				1
preposed adjectives	PAdj				1
pronouns	PN		1		
articles	ART		1		
connectors	Conn		1		1

continued…

Table 10. Grammatical complexity frequencies: Number of studies by type of result (cont.)

measure	code	***	**	*	X
transitional connectors	TConn				1
subordinating connectors	SConn				1
coordinating connectors	CConn			1	1

*** Developmental measures that highly correlate with proficiency (r=.65+), or show an overall effect for proficiency (p<.05) together with a significant difference between three or more adjacent proficiency levels (p<.05).

** Developmental measures that moderately correlate with proficiency (r=.45–.64), or show an overall effect for proficiency for two or more proficiency levels (p<.05).

* Developmental measures that weakly correlate with proficiency (r=.25–.44), or show a trend towards an effect for proficiency (p<.10).

X Developmental measures that show no correlation with or effect for proficiency.

Reduced clauses (RedC)

RedC = total number of reductions of original sentences to less than a clause

***	Monroe 75
**	
*	
X	

Monroe (1975), in his study of writers learning French as a foreign language, found that when a simplified passage was rewritten, a count of the number of reduced clauses (RedC) significantly discriminated between the three advanced school levels. Because of these results, he proposed three developmental stages in the grammatical development of second language writing: 1) coordination of clauses, 2) subordination of clauses, 3) reduction of multiple clauses to a single clause. An illustration of these three stages is provided by Monroe (1975, p. 1026):

Sentences: J'ai un fils. Il a dix ans. ("I have a son. He is ten.")

Stage 1: J'ai un fils et il a dix ans. ("I have a son and he is ten.")

Stage 2: J'ai un fils qui a dix ans. ("I have a son who is ten.")

Stage 3: J'ai un fils agé de dix ans. ("I have a ten-year-old son.")

However, this measure can be applied only to rewriting tasks, the only context in which it is possible to know the number of clauses being manipulated by the writer.

Dependent clauses (DepC)
DepC = total number of dependent clauses

***	
**	Homburg 84: analysis 1
*	Homburg 84: analysis 2
X	Kameen 79

Both Homburg (1984) and Kameen (1979) counted the number of dependent clauses (DepC) in second language writing. Kameen defined dependent clauses as adverbial, adjectival, and nominal, while Homburg defined them as subordinate and relative. In Homburg's study of three levels of holistic ratings, he found that the number of dependent clauses increased steadily between the three levels, significantly discriminating between the highest and lowest group (analysis 1). In a discriminant analysis, he also found that this measure was a discriminating factor that correlated with program level (analysis 2). On the other hand, Kameen (1979) found that what he called 'secondary' clauses did not significantly distinguish z-scores that were compared by a Wilcoxin signed rank test. In fact, he says that the "commonly-held intuition that 'good' writers have a superior command of the use of subordinate clauses . . . is in no way supported by this study" (p. 347). However, in Kameen's study, the 'good' writers produced an average of 11 dependent clauses per composition, whereas the 'poor' writers produced an average of 9.10 per composition, although the difference was not significant.

Passives (Pass)
Pass = total number of passives

***	
**	Kameen 79
*	
X	

Kameen (1979) counted the number of passives (Pass) that occurred in the writing of two groups that were separated into 'good' and 'poor' writers based on holistic ratings, and found that it significantly differentiated the two proficiency groups. Kameen, following native language studies (e.g., Hunt, 1965), counted the incidence of dynamic passives (e.g., They were given the notice and He had been told to sit down), but not stative passives (e.g., I am interested in the results and My coat is torn), in his analysis (Kameen, 1979, p. 344). Kameen suggested that "higher incidence of passive voice indicates a greater control over the syntactic structures of the language" (p. 349).

Passive sentences (PassS)

PassS = total number of sentences with one or more passives

***	
**	Kameen 79; Kawata 92
*	
X	

In a variant of the passive measure, Kameen (1979) and Kawata (1992) counted the number of sentences that had one or more passives in them (PassS). Kameen found that this measure was significantly related to two widely-spaced levels based on holistic ratings, and Kawata found that this measure was related to grades assigned to high school juniors. Kameen also used two other passive frequency measures — number of passives in main clauses and number of passives in secondary clauses — both of which significantly differentiated Kameen's two groups. Kameen (1979, pp. 348–349) points out that despite the widespread belief that "the use of passive voice leads to ineffective writing," passive measures have been useful in some native language studies (Hunt, 1965) as well as in his study.

Adverbial clauses (AdvC)

AdvC = total number of adverbial clauses

***	
**	
*	
X	Kameen 79

Kameen (1979) counted the number of adverbial clauses (AdvC) in the timed compositions of two groups of writers, and found that this measure was not significantly related to holistic ratings of those writers, although the 'good' writers produced more adverbial clauses than the 'poor' writers. He did not define what he meant by adverbial clauses, that is, whether they included participle phrases or not.

Adjective clauses (AdjC)

AdjC = total number of adjective clauses

***	
**	
*	
X	Kameen 79, Sharma 80

Kameen (1979) also counted the number of adjective clauses (AdjC) in the timed compositions of two groups of writers, and found that this measure was not significantly related to holistic ratings of those writers, although the 'good' writers produced more adjective clauses than the 'poor' writers. Sharma (1980) compared the number of relative clauses (adjective clauses) for low intermediate and advanced learners using a rewriting task. In Sharma's study, the number of relative clauses decreased for the advanced learners, which Sharma suggests is because they were at a stage of reducing relatives to other types of modification. However, he found no significant difference between the two groups in the number of relative clauses.

Nominal clauses (NomC)

NomC = total number of nominal clauses

***	
**	
*	
X	Kameen 79

Kameen (1979) also counted the number of nominal clauses (NomC) in the timed compositions of two groups of writers, and found that this measure was not significantly related to holistic ratings of those writers, although the 'good' writers produced more nominal clauses than the 'poor' writers. He did not define what he meant by nominal clauses, that is, whether he included gerund and infinitive phrases or not.

Prepositional phrases (PP)

PP = total number of prepositional phrases

***	
**	
*	
X	Sharma 80

A count of the number of prepositional phrases (PP) was used by Sharma (1980), who used a rewriting task to compare low intermediate and advanced learners. An increase in prepositional phrases would be an indicator of the reduction of adverbial or relative clauses to prepositional phrases, as Monroe (1975) proposed as an advanced stage. However, Sharma found no significant difference between the two groups in the number of prepositional phrases. Since Sharma used a rewriting task, perhaps he should have considered all clause reductions as a group, as Monroe (1975) did, rather than separating them by type.

Preposed adjectives (PAdj)

PAdj = total number of preposed adjectives

***	
**	
*	
X	Sharma 80

Sharma (1980) also counted the number of preposed adjectives (PAdj) using a rewriting task to compare low intermediate and advanced learners. An increase in preposed adjectives would be a sign of the transition from subordination to reducing subordinations to phrases or words, creating more 'complex nominals' (Yau, 1991). However, he found no significant difference between the two groups in the number of preposed adjectives.

Pronouns (PN)

PN = total number of all types of pronouns

***	
**	Evola et al. 80: analysis 1
*	
X	

In a different approach, Evola et al. (1980: analysis 1) counted the total number of pronouns (PN) in second language writing samples, and found that the number of pronouns significantly discriminated between five program levels, although not between adjacent levels.

Articles (ART)

ART = total number of all types of articles

***	
**	Evola et al. 80: analysis 1
*	
X	

Evola et al. (1980: analysis 1) also counted the total number of articles (ART) in second language writing samples, and found that the number of articles significantly discriminated between five program levels, although not between adjacent levels.

Connectors (Conn)

Conn = total number of all types of connectors

***	
**	Evola et al. 80: analysis 1
*	
X	Homburg 84: analysis 1

Both Evola et al. (1980: analysis 1) and Homburg (1984: analysis 1) counted the total number of connectors (Conn) in second language writing samples. Evola et al. found that the number of connectors significantly discriminated between five program levels, although not between adjacent levels. However, Homburg found no significant differences between three holistic rating levels in the number of connectors. Presumably, the presence of connectors is related to issues in coordination and subordination, but exactly how remains unclear.

Transitional connectors (TConn)

TConn = total number of transitional connectors

***	
**	
*	
X	Homburg 84: analysis 1

Homburg (1984: analysis 1) counted the total number of transitional connectors (TConn) in second language writing samples, and found that the number of transitional connectors did not significantly discriminate among three holistic rating levels. Homburg defined transitional connectors as connectors such as subsequently, therefore, however, and also.

Subordinating connectors (SConn)

SConn = total number of subordinating connectors

***	
**	
*	
X	Homburg 84: analysis 1

Homburg (1984: analysis 1) also counted the total number of subordinating connectors (SConn) in second language writing samples, and found that the number of subordinating connectors did not significantly discriminate among three holistic rating levels. Homburg defined subordinating connectors as connectors such as when, before, because, and although.

Coordinating connectors (CConn)

CConn = total number of coordinating connectors

***	
**	
*	Homburg 84: analysis 2
X	Homburg 84: analysis 1

Homburg (1984) also counted the total number of coordinating connectors (CConn) in second language writing samples, defining coordinating connectors as connectors such as *for, so, but, yet, or, nor*, and *and.* Homburg found that the number of coordinating connectors did not significantly discriminate among three holistic rating levels (analysis 1), with level 5 producing an average of 6.20 coordinating connectors per composition, level 6 producing an average of 8.00, but level 7 producing an average of 5.10. When these figures are divided by the average number of T-units each group produced, the trend is still the same (from .34 to .39 to .28). This increase at an intermediate level and then decrease at a higher level is similar to Bardovi-Harlig's (1992) results for a coordination index, Ishikawa's (1995) results for the clauses per T-unit coordination ratio, and Sharma's (1980) results for coordinate clauses per T-unit. This is consistent with the proposal that there may be an early increase in coordination followed by a later decline. In a discriminant analysis (analysis 2), Homburg did find that coordinating connectors were one of the factors that accounted for variance, with a weak correlation between this measure and program level.

GRAMMATICAL COMPLEXITY RATIOS

There are various types of grammatical complexity ratios that measure the relationship between clauses, sentences, and T-units. One type are the general complexity measures (clauses per T-unit and clauses per sentence), which consider the proportion of all clause types to a larger unit such as the sentence or T-unit. Another type are the dependent clause measures (adverbial clauses per T-unit, dependent clauses per clause, dependent clauses per T-unit, dependent infinitives per T-unit), which consider the relationship between dependent and independent clauses. A third type are the coordination measures (T-units per sentence, coordinate clauses or coordinate phrases per T-unit), which consider the relationship between coordination and independent clauses.

Table 11 presents the results for the various grammatical complexity ratios that have been used in studies of second language writing development. As can be seen in the table, many of the measures have been used in only a few studies, though one measure, a T-unit complexity ratio (the number of clauses per T-unit, or C/T) has been used in 17 studies, although with mixed findings. A closer analysis of the results reveals that the T-unit complexity ratio does generally progress with proficiency level regardless of how proficiency is defined, although there may be adjacent levels which are undifferentiated by this measure. However, for measures that attempt to tap into coordination, there are predominantly non-significant results, particularly for the T-unit coordination ratio (the number of T-units per sentence, or T/S).

Other notable results include Hirano's (1991) finding that a dependent clause per clause ratio (DC/C) does significantly differentiate three program levels based on CELT scores, and Homburg's (1984) finding that a dependent clause per T-unit ratio (DC/T) significantly distinguished three holistic rating levels that had high reliability. However, Kameen (1979) did not find a significant relationship between dependent clauses per clause (DC/C) and holistic ratings differentiating 'poor' and 'good' writers, nor did Vann (1979) find a significant relationship between dependent clauses per T-unit (DC/T) and holistic ratings of writers. This suggests that the proportion of dependent clauses may be related to general language proficiency but not necessarily to teachers' judgments. Finally, measures of the number of complex nominals (Cooper, 1976) and passives (Kameen, 1979) do seem to capture aspects of writing that are related to both school level and holistic ratings.

Table 11. Grammatical complexity ratios: Number of studies by type of result

measure	code	***	**	*	X
T-unit complexity ratio	C/T	1	6	4	7
sentence complexity ratio	C/S		1		1
clauses per error-free T-unit	C/EFT				2
dependent clause ratio	DC/C	1		1	1
dependent clauses per T-unit	DC/T		1		2
adverbial clauses per T-unit	AdvC/T				1
complex T-unit ratio	CT/T			1	
sentence coordination ratio	T/S		1		4
coordinate clauses per T-unit	CC/T				1
coordinate phrases per T-unit	CP/T			1	
dependent infinitives per T-unit	DI/T				1
complex nominals per T-unit	CN/T		1		

continued...

Table 11. Grammatical complexity ratios: Number of studies by type of result (cont.)

measure	code	***	**	*	X
passives per T-unit	P/T		1		
passives per clause	P/C		1		
passives per sentence	P/S		1		

*** Developmental measures that highly correlate with proficiency (r=.65+), or show an overall effect for proficiency (p<.05) together with a significant difference between three or more adjacent proficiency levels (p<.05).

** Developmental measures that moderately correlate with proficiency (r=.45–.64), or show an overall effect for proficiency for two or more proficiency levels (p<.05).

* Developmental measures that weakly correlate with proficiency (r=.25–.44), or show a trend towards an effect for proficiency (p<.10).

X Developmental measures that show no correlation with or effect for proficiency.

T-unit complexity ratio (C/T)
C/T = total number of clauses divided by total number of T-units

***	Hirano 91: analysis 2
**	Cooper 76; Flahive & Snow 80: analysis 2-level 1, level 2, level 3, level 6; Monroe 75
*	Casanave 94; Flahive & Snow 80: analysis 1, analysis 2-level 5; Hirano 91: analysis 1
X	Bardovi-Harlig & Bofman 89; Flahive & Snow 80: analysis 2-level 4; Ishikawa 95: analysis 1–group 1, group 2; Kameen 79; Perkins 80; Sharma 80

The measure of the number of clauses as a ratio to the number of T-units (C/T) was called a subordination ratio by Hunt (1965). Hunt called this a subordinate clause index following LaBrant's (1934) usage, but differed in his method of calculation. Hunt divided the total number of clauses by the number of main clauses (T-units), while LaBrant divided the number of subordinate clauses by the total number of clauses (Hunt, 1965, p. 33). LaBrant's calculation is indeed a subordinate clause ratio, but Hunt's method of calculation is a T-unit complexity ratio, because what is being measured in the clause depth of the T-unit.

Hunt defines clauses as "a structure with a subject and a finite verb" (p. 15). This definition of clause includes independent/main clauses, as well as three types of subordinate clauses: adverbial clauses, adjective/relative clauses, and nominal clauses. In contrast, Bardovi-Harlig and Bofman (1989) equated clauses with non-finite verb phrases, which not only would include these four clause types, but also participle, gerund, and infinitive verb phrases. When it comes to calculating clauses per T-unit (C/T), for Hunt, 'C' means four clause types, for Bardovi-Harlig, 'C' means seven clause types.

A T-unit contains one independent clause plus any number of other types of clauses, including adverbial, adjective, and nominal clauses, which this measure captures. A T-unit complexity ratio of 2.0 would mean that, on average, each T-unit consists of one independent clause plus one other clause, for a ratio of two to one. Because in second language development, not all students may use tense markers or subjects, we feel that including both finite and non-finite verb phrases as in Bardovi-Harlig and Bofman (1989) is important for the reliability of judgments. In effect, it would really be a verb phrases per T-unit (VP/T) measure. It might be useful to compare whether measuring clauses per T-unit (C/T) or verb phrases per T-unit (VP/T) is more revealing.

The T-unit complexity ratio is designed to measure how grammatically complex the writing of a learner is, under the assumption that the more clauses there are per T-unit, the more complex the writing is. However, in second language studies, seven studies found a significant relationship between proficiency and the T-unit complexity ratio, while eleven did not. Hirano (1991) found a relationship between program level and clauses per T-unit (analysis 2), but not between CELT scores and clauses per T-unit (analysis 1). Cooper (1976) and Monroe (1975) found a relationship between school level and clauses per T-unit. Flahive and Snow (1980: analysis 2) found a relationship between holistic ratings and clauses per T-unit for the first, second, third, and sixth program levels, but not for the fourth or fifth levels. Bardovi-Harlig and Bofman (1989) and Perkins (1980) didn't find a relationship between clauses per T-unit and pass/fail ratings of advanced learners; nor did Ishikawa (1995) find a relationship between clauses per T-unit and pre- and post-tests with two groups of beginning learners. Casanave (1994) found an overall increase in clauses per T-unit after three semesters of journal writing, but didn't test the differences statistically, so we are treating her results as a trend. Neither Kameen (1979) nor Sharma (1980) found a relationship between clauses per T-unit and low-intermediate versus advanced groups determined by holistic ratings.

It appears that the clauses per T-unit measure is most related to program or school level than to short-term change in classes or holistic ratings of samples. However, in all of these studies except Casanave (1994) and Perkins (1980), the clauses per T-unit measure increased with proficiency level regardless of how proficiency was defined, and whether or not the increase was significant. In some cases, the middle levels were undifferentiated (Monroe, 1975; Cooper, 1976), but there was a general progression upward from low to intermediate to advanced levels. In Flahive and Snow (1980), although the first five levels gradually progressed from 1.07 clauses per T-unit to 1.92 clauses per T-unit, at level six the ratio dropped to 1.74, but that doesn't happen in the other studies. Only Perkins (1980) found an inverse progression of clauses per T-unit relative to holistic ratings, when he compared pass (1.5 C/T), pass minus (1.64 C/T), and fail (1.65 C/T) ratings of advanced writers in a single class. In an analysis of individual learners' journal entries, Casanave (1994) found that some learners vacillated in clauses per T-unit over time. A comparison of the means across studies shows that there is a range from 1.07 clauses per T-unit for the lowest level learners to 2.17 for the most advanced (but note that Casanave's 1994 means do not fall in this pattern, suggesting that learners produced less than one clause per T-unit, which is an impossibility).

This apparent general progression in clauses per T-unit isn't consistent with the claim of Monroe (1975) and Sharma (1980) that there is a stage of reduction from clauses to phrases that yields a lower clauses per T-unit ratio at advanced levels, particularly since in their studies the advanced levels did have a higher clause per T-unit ratio. Cooper (1976) and Flahive and Snow (1980) have also suggested that this measure cannot discriminate at higher proficiency levels, because Cooper's third through fifth-year German students were undifferentiated statistically (from 1.2 clauses per T-unit for sophomores, to 1.4–1.5 clauses per T-unit for juniors to graduate students, to 1.7 clauses per T-unit for native speakers), and Flahive and Snow found that their sixth level dropped in clauses per T-unit even though the five lower levels did gradually progress. However, it seems to us that the majority of results do support the usefulness of the clauses per T-unit measure (including the progression for five of the levels in Flahive & Snow's study), since six other studies found that the direction of difference based on proficiency level is linear and progressive (Bardovi-Harlig & Bofman, 1989; Hirano, 1991; Ishikawa, 1995; Kameen, 1979; Monroe, 1975; Sharma, 1980).

Sentence complexity ratio (C/S)
C/S = total number of sentences divided by total number of clauses

***	
**	Ishikawa 95: analysis 1–group 2
*	
X	Ishikawa 95: analysis 1–group 1

Ishikawa (1995) investigated the ratio of clauses to sentences (C/S) in a sentence complexity ratio, which is a variation of the T-unit complexity ratio discussed above. She used sentences as the unit of analysis because her beginning level writers sometimes divided what would be considered a single T-unit into separate sentences, beginning new sentences with subordinators (e.g., I went to school. Because I had to.). She thought that the sentence-level complexity measure might be more indicative of developmental growth over three months, because it would reveal growth in the ability to combine clauses within a single sentence, whether from coordination or subordination. Ishikawa found that there was a significant increase in clauses per sentence for one of her groups but not the other, although both groups progressed in clauses per sentence (from 1.41 to 1.68 clauses per sentence for group 1, and 1.60 to 1.68 clauses per sentence for group 2). Bardovi-Harlig (1992) also argues that the sentence might be a better comparative unit for measuring complexity for adult learners. Using sentences as a production unit captures the ways that learners coordinate, subordinate, and reduce their thoughts within a single unit that has psychological reality for them.

Clauses per error-free T-unit (C/EFT)

C/EFT = total number of clauses divided by total number of error-free T-units

***	
**	
*	
X	Perkins & Leahy 80: analysis 1, analysis 2

Perkins and Leahy (1980: analysis 2) investigated the relationship between grades in a course and the number of clauses divided by the number of error-free T-units (C/EFT). They assumed that the presence of more clauses in error-free T-units would indicate greater language development, but they found no significant relationship between the measure and grades (analysis 2); those with an A grade averaged 1.3 clauses per error-free T-unit but those with a B grade averaged 1.4 clauses per error-free T-unit. They also found no significant difference between native speakers and second language writers on this measure (analysis 1), since both groups had average clauses per error-free T-unit ratios of 1.4. This does not necessarily mean that the clauses per error-free T-unit measure is a bad one, since Perkins and Leahy compared it to the grades for take-home essays of very advanced writers, which can be influenced by all kinds of other factors including the number of sources referenced, careful versus careless editing, or perceived effort, among other things.

Despite the accuracy issue in the use of the error-free T-unit as the production unit for this measure, we are treating this as a complexity measure because what it measures is how complex the units are, that is, how many clauses per unit there are. This is similar to the justification for treating words per error-free T-unit (W/EFT) as a fluency measure, since it measures how long the units are. Neither of these measures indicate how accurate the writing is. For example, if a writer produced only one error-free T-unit out of 30 total T-units, and that T-unit happened to be very complex, that writer's clauses per error-free T-unit (C/EFT) ratio would be high; if it happened to be very long, that writer's words per error-free T-unit (W/EFT) ratio would be high. Neither of these measures would reveal the lack of accurate T-units in the writing.

Dependent Clause Ratio (DC/C)

DC/C = total number of dependent clauses divided by total number of clauses

***	Hirano 91: analysis 2
**	
*	Hirano 91: analysis 1
X	Kameen 79

The dependent clause ratio is a measure that examines the degree of embedding in a text, by counting the number of dependent clauses as a percentage of the total number of clauses (DC/C). Hirano (1991) did not define what she meant by dependent clauses, and although Kameen (1979) did not explicitly say what he meant by 'secondary clauses,' he implied in his discussion that they include adverbial, adjective, and nominal clauses (p. 347). Hirano's (1991) study is interesting because she found that this measure significantly differentiated all three program levels based on CELT score ranges (analysis 2), but only weakly correlated with CELT scores themselves (analysis 1). She consistently found this type of result for many measures, which means that the actual scores were not directly related to a measure such as this, but that writers with roughly the same proficiency range did have something in common on this and other measures. Her three groups ranged from averages of .18 (low) to .25 (mid) to .33 (high) dependent clauses per T-unit.

However, Kameen (1979) didn't find a significant difference between two groups based on holistic ratings of their writing (.40 dependent clauses per clause for the 'good' writers and .37 for the 'poor' writers). Kameen, based on the lack of discrimination of both dependent clauses per clause (DC/C) and clauses per T-unit (C/T) coupled with the significance of both words per T-unit (W/T) and words per clause (W/C), suggests that good writers produce longer T-units as a result of using more words rather than more clauses, most likely because they reduce clauses to prepositional, infinitive and participle phrases.

Dependent clauses per T-unit (DC/T)

DC/T = total number of dependent clauses divided by number of T-units	
***	
**	Homburg 84: analysis 1
*	
X	Vann 79: analysis 1, analysis 2

Vann (1979) and Homburg (1984: analysis 1) measured the number of dependent clauses per T-unit (DC/T), yet another variation of a clause embedding measure. Vann did not define dependent clause in her analysis, but Homburg defined dependent clauses as instances of relativization and subordination (p. 92). In a study of 30-minute essays, Homburg found a significant relationship between this measure and holistic rating level, with level five having a dependent clauses per T-unit ratio of .38, level six a ratio of .54, and level seven a ratio of .60. However, in a study of timed written responses to a silent film, Vann (1979) found no significant relationship between holistic ratings of the writing samples and this measure (analysis 2), nor did she find that dependent clauses per T-unit was a discriminant factor in a multiple regression step analysis based on TOEFL score (analysis 1). Vann doesn't provide the ratio means on which the analyses are based.

Adverbial clauses per T-unit (AdvC/T)

AdvC/T = total number of adverbial clauses divided by total number of T-units

***	
**	
*	
X	Cooper 76

Cooper (1976) tabulated the number of adverbial clauses per T-unit (AdvC/T) in his study of German as a foreign language, using 10 T-unit samples from each writer. He counted adverbial clauses as clauses headed by time, place, cause, and condition subordinators. Scores on this measure should increase as learners move from coordination to subordination; however, Cooper found that the relationship between school level and this measure were non-significant. He did find a progression in the ratio based on level, however, with sophomores producing .13 adverbial clauses per T-unit, juniors producing .14, seniors producing .15, graduate students producing .18, and native speakers producing .25. In future studies, not only this measure but also a measure of the number of adverbial clauses per clause (AdvC/C) might be considered.

Complex T-unit ratio (CT/T)

CT/T = total number of complex T-units divided by total number of T-units

***	
**	
*	Casanave 94
X	

Casanave (1994) found an overall increase in the number of complex T-units per T-unit (CT/T) in journal entries written over a three-semester period, but didn't measure the increase statistically. She counted complex T-units as those that contained either a dependent or embedded clause. In an analysis of individual learners' journal entries, she found that some learners vacillated in complex T-units per T-unit over time. In the individual student patterns, the ratio of complex T-units per T-unit varied from .036 to .478, which means that anywhere from none to a half of the T-units in any particular sample had at least one embedded or dependent clause.

Sentence coordination ratio (T/S)

T/S = total number of T-units divided by total number of sentences

***	
**	Monroe 75
*	
X	Cooper 76; Homburg 84: analysis 1; Ishikawa 95: analysis 1–group 1, group 2

A sentence coordination ratio, which is the number of T-units divided by the number of sentences (T/S), was employed by Hunt (1965) in order to show the decrease of run-on sentences as grade-school children become more proficient in writing. At the earlier stages, T-units are connected by coordination to make longer sentences. As clauses become incorporated into a single T-unit through subordination, T-units get longer, but there would be fewer of them per sentence. Therefore, T-units per sentence (T/S) should decline as clauses per T-unit (C/T) increases. However, in second language studies, the T-units per sentence measure has not been shown to be very useful. Only Monroe (1975) found a significant relationship between university school level and the T-unit coordination ratio, with the number of T-units per sentence declining from 1.37 for freshmen to 1.10 for the native language comparison group.

Although the difference was non-significant, the two groups of beginning level writers in Ishikawa (1995) increased their coordination of sentences from .95 and .97 to 1.06 and 1.09 after instruction, which may indicate that early development proceeds from uncoordinated clauses to coordinated clauses. However, neither Cooper (1976) nor Homburg (1984) found even the expected direction of difference based on school or holistic rating level, with Cooper's subjects hovering around 1.2 T-units per sentence at all levels, and Homburg's subjects ranging from 1.35 to 1.59 T-units per sentence, but not related to level. Whether there is an early increase in coordination that then gradually declines and is variable depending on the writing task is a matter that requires further investigation.

Coordinate clauses per T-unit (CC/T)

CC/T = total number of coordinate clauses divided by total number of T-units

***	
**	
*	
X	Sharma 80

Sharma (1980) measured the number of coordinate clauses as a percentage of the number of T-units (CC/T). This measure was intended capture the number of coordinations between clauses just as the T-unit coordination measure (T/S) does. Sharma's assumption was that this measure would decrease as writers become more proficient and move from coordination to subordination. However, Sharma didn't find a significant difference on this measure between low and advanced program levels when he had them rewrite the 'aluminum' passage created by O'Donnell et al. (1967) and used by Hunt (1970). He found that low intermediate learners used .37 coordinate clauses per T-unit, high intermediate learners .52, but advanced learners .43. This shows an increase followed by a decline, which is consistent with Homburg's (1984) results for the number of coordinating connectors discussed in the last section.

Coordinate phrases per T-unit (CP/T)

CP/T = total number of phrases with coordinators divided by total number of T-units

***	
**	
*	Cooper 76
X	

Cooper (1976) tabulated the number of coordinate phrases per T-unit (CP/T) in his study of German as a foreign language, using samples of ten T-units from each writer. In his definition of coordinate phrases, Cooper (1976) included adjective and adverb phrases (e.g., adjective phrases: *frisches, weisses Brot* 'fresh, white bread'; adverb phrases: *lief schnell und vorsichtig* 'ran quickly and carefully'), noun phrases (e.g., *der Mann und die Frau* 'the man and woman'), and verb phrases (e.g., *er liest und schreibt* 'he reads and writes'). So, the coordinate phrase ratio captures one means by which clauses and T-units get lengthened, by coordinating the phrases contained within the clause or T-unit. Here, the type of coordination being considered occurs within clauses, not across clause or T-unit boundaries. Cooper (1976) found only a trend towards a relationship between coordinate phrases and school level, with second-year students producing .42 coordinate phrases per T-unit, third-year students declining to .24, fourth-year students staying at .28, fifth-year students increasing to .44, and native speakers producing .72. Cooper mixes quite different types of coordination in his measure, which may explain the variance in the results. Distinctions between types of coordination and the use of clauses as the unit of measurement (coordinate phrases per clause; CP/C) might improve the results. At any rate, Cooper does show a linear progression by means of this measure that suggests that there is a later reduction stage.

Dependent infinitives per T-unit (DI/T)

DI/T = total number of dependent infinitives divided by total number of T-units

***	
**	
*	
X	Cooper 76

Cooper (1976) counted the number of dependent infinitives that occurred as a percentage of the number of T-units (DI/T) in a study of written texts in German as a foreign language, using samples of ten T-units from each writer. According to Cooper (1976, p. 181), dependent infinitives are "near sentence embeddings" such as modal verbs plus infinitives, "second-prong infinitives" (e.g., *er hat etwas zu tun* 'he has something to do'), and "end-field infinitives" (e.g., *er hat aufgehort, Zigaretten zu rauchen* 'he stopped smoking cigarettes'). He included infinitives that function as nominals in his nominal measure (see below) but not here. He found that dependent infinitives per T-unit increased gradually with increasing school level, but that the measure did not significantly discriminate among school levels, although the ratio of dependent infinitives to T-units increased gradually from .21 for second-year students to .28 for fifth-year students, with .36 produced by native speakers. The use of clauses as the denominator (dependent infinitives per clause; DI/C) might yield an even better result, because a clause count doesn't differentiate between coordination and subordination like a T-unit count does, a distinction that isn't relevant to this measure.

Complex nominals per T-unit (CN/T)

CN/T = total number of complex nominals divided by total number of T-units

***	
**	Cooper 76
*	
X	

Cooper (1976) also measured the number of complex nominals per T-unit (CN/T) in his study of German as a foreign language, using samples of ten T-units from each writer. He defined two types of nominals: headed nominals (nouns plus adjectives or relative clauses), and non-headed nominals (noun clauses, gerunds, and infinitives). This notion of complex nominals is similar to Yau's (1991) definition of complex nominals, except that Cooper, unlike Yau, included noun clauses that were direct objects of verbs. Hunt (1965) had found that the frequency of complex nominals increased with the age of the writer. Cooper also found that this measure was significantly related to school level, and scores increased as level increased, from .81 for sophomores, to 1.55 for juniors, 1.89 for seniors, 2.62 for graduate students, and 3.26 for native speakers. He attributes this to "the writer's ability to pack more information into sentences and T-units by lengthening independent clauses" (Cooper, 1976, p. 183), which corresponds to Monroe's (1975) concept of packing sentences into clauses as a process of reduction. The use of clauses as the denominator (complex nominals per clause; CN/C) might yield an even better result, because a clause count doesn't differentiate between coordination and subordination like a T-unit count does, a distinction that isn't relevant to this measure.

Passives per T-unit (P/T)

P/T = total number of passives divided by total number of T-units

***	
**	Kameen 79
*	
X	

Kameen (1979) counted the number of passives per T-unit (P/T) that occurred in the writing of two groups that were separated into 'good' and 'poor' writers based on holistic ratings, and found that it significantly differentiated the two proficiency groups. The 'good' writers had .20 passives per T-unit compared to .05 passives per T-unit for the 'poor' writers. Kameen, following native language studies (e.g., Hunt, 1965), counted the incidence of 'dynamic passives' (e.g., They were given the notice and He had been told to sit down), but not 'stative passives' (e.g., I am interested in the results and My coat is torn) in his analysis (Kameen, 1979, p. 344). It is not clear where the use of passives fits in second language development, but Kameen suggests that "higher incidence of passive voice indicates a greater control over the syntactic structures of the language" (p. 349).

Passives per clause (P/C)

P/C = total number of passives divided by total number of clauses

***	
**	Kameen 79
*	
X	

Kameen (1979) also counted the number of passives per clause (P/C) that occurred in the writing of two groups that were separated into 'good' and 'poor' writers based on holistic ratings, and found that it significantly differentiated the two proficiency groups. The 'good' writers had .12 passives per clause compared to .03 passives per clause for the 'poor' writers.

Passives per sentence (P/S)

P/S = total number of passives divided by total number of sentences

***	
**	Kameen 79
*	
X	

Kameen (1979) also counted the number of passives per sentence (P/S) that occurred in the writing of two groups that were separated into 'good' and 'poor' writers based on holistic ratings, and found that it significantly differentiated the two proficiency groups. The 'good' writers had .24 passives per sentence compared to .06 passives per sentence for the 'poor' writers.

GRAMMATICAL COMPLEXITY INDICES

None of the three grammatical complexity indices proposed by researchers significantly relate to second language development, as shown in Table 12 below. One of these measures, the coordination index, is a variant of the subordination/coordination ratio measures discussed in the last section, while the other two, the complexity formula and complexity index, weigh the structures present in the writing on the basis of a pre-determined scale of complexity. However, most of these studies investigated groups of learners at the same general program level (Casanave, 1994; Flahive & Snow, 1980: analysis 2; Perkins, 1980; Tapia, 1993), and that may explain the non-significant results. Flahive and Snow (1980: analysis 1) did not find the complexity index a discriminant factor between three program levels, but they did not look at how strongly it may or may not have correlated with level. Although Bardovi-Harlig did not do a statistical test of the relationship between program level and the coordination index, she did find a promising trend.

Table 12. Grammatical complexity indices: Number of studies by type of result

measure	code	***	**	*	X
coordination index	CoordIndex			1	2
complexity formula	ComplexFormula				1
complexity index	ComplexIndex			3	5

*** Developmental measures that highly correlate with proficiency (r=.65+), or show an overall effect for proficiency (p<.05) together with a significant difference between three or more adjacent proficiency levels (p<.05).

** Developmental measures that moderately correlate with proficiency (r=.45–.64), or show an overall effect for proficiency for two or more proficiency levels (p<.05).

* Developmental measures that weakly correlate with proficiency (r=.25–.44), or show a trend towards an effect for proficiency (p<.10).

X Developmental measures that show no correlation with or effect for proficiency.

Coordination index (CoordIndex)

CoordIndex = number of independent clause coordinations divided by total number of combined clauses (clauses minus sentences)

***		
**		
*	Bardovi-Harlig 92	
X	Casanave 94; Tapia 93	

This index measure was proposed by Bardovi-Harlig (1992) as an alternative to an analysis of the number of T-units per sentence (T/S) as a measure of coordination, in order to distinguish between learners who use coordination versus subordination to increase sentence complexity. The coordination index is calculated by dividing the total number of independent clause coordinations by the total number of combined clauses, which are the number of clauses minus the number of sentences. Subtracting the number of sentences from the number of clauses yields a count of all subordinated and coordinated clauses. In effect, Bardovi-Harlig is dividing the number of coordinated clauses by the total number of both subordinated and coordinated clauses. This index captures the ratio of coordinate clauses relative to all combined clauses, and it should decrease as learners move from coordination to subordination.

Unfortunately, Bardovi-Harlig (1992) did not conduct a statistical test of the relationship between this measure and seven program levels, but she did find a regular decrease in the score for all levels except for level six, which increased. Because of the promising nature of her results, we decided to treat them as a developmental trend. However, this measure was not significant for Tapia's (1993) comparison of levels five and six out of the same seven-level program, nor did it appear to progress linearly in Casanave's (1994) analysis of the journal entries of five students over three semesters. In Table 13 is a comparison of Bardovi-Harlig and Tapia's results, which show a clear progression of decreasing coordination with program level, although the writers between levels 4 and 7 have perhaps reached a floor on this measure. Hunt (1965, p. 103) acknowledged that "due perhaps to constraints of English prose style, a greatly expanded use of subordinate clause additions is limited." However, Sharma (1980) and Homburg (1984) also found an increase in the number of coordinate clauses per T-unit at intermediate levels with a drop at advanced levels, so there may be a developmental reason for a relatively late increase and then drop.

Table 13. Coordination index means

	Tapia	Bardovi-Harlig
level 1	.40	
level 2	.36	
level 3	.29	
level 4	.15	
level 5	.15	.12
level 6	.10	.18
level 7	.10	

It would of course be possible to develop a mirror-image subordination index, which would be the total number of subordinate clauses divided by the total number of combined clauses. The subordination index would be expected to increase as language development advances, although the possibility of the reduction of clauses to phrases might make this measure non-linear.

Complexity formula (ComplexFormula)
ComplexFormula = score of weighted structures divided by number of sentences

***	
**	
*	
X	Perkins 80

This syntactic complexity formula was developed by Botel, Dawkins and Granowsky (1973) based on transformational grammar, experimental data from children's processing of syntactic structures, and studies of children's development of oral and written language. In this index, various grammatical structures are weighted as 0, 1, 2, or 3 according to their syntactic complexity. For example, simple sentences (e.g., he went) are assigned a 0; noun modifiers (e.g., the big man ate here) are assigned a 1; passive sentences (e.g., the ball was hit by Bob) are assigned a 2; noun clauses used as subjects (e.g., that he eats is important) are assigned a 3. Perkins (1980) found that when he compared holistic ratings of the writing of advanced learners to scores on the complexity formula there was no significant relationship. However, the lack of significant results may have resulted because his groups were at the same general proficiency level, or because holistic ratings are not related to the presence of these types of structures. Although the transformational theory that the weightings are based on is outdated, the attempt to develop a theory-driven weighting of structures is a welcome addition to the analysis of the development of grammatical complexity.

Complexity index (ComplexIndex)
ComplexIndex = sum of T-unit scores divided by number of T-units
T-unit score = score of weighted structures plus number of words in T-unit
divided by number of words in T-unit

***	
**	
*	Flahive & Snow 80: analysis 2-level 1, level 2, level 6
X	Flahive & Snow 80: analysis 1, analysis 2-level 3, level 4, level 5; Perkins 80

Another type of complexity index was developed by Flahive and Snow (1980), who adapted Endicott's (1973) measure of morphological and transformational complexity, and assigned points to grammatical structures on the basis of how often they appeared in the writing of advanced second language learners. Flahive and Snow assigned a value of 3 to adverbial and noun clauses, a value of 2 to relative clauses, passives, embedded questions, possessives and comparatives, and a value of 1 to each derivational morpheme and each adjective. Additionally, a value of 1 was assigned to each word. These values were added up for each T-unit, the sum of which was divided by the total number of words in that T-unit. All of the T-unit scores were then added together and divided by the number of total T-units in the writing. This means that regardless of T-unit length, each T-unit carries the same weight when it comes to determining an average complexity score. A different calculation would be to add together all of the weighted structures plus the total number of words and then divide by the total number of words. That would provide a measure of how many complex structures appeared per words, as opposed to T-units.

In a statistical analysis, the complexity index was not significantly related to holistic ratings of compositions written by learners at the same general proficiency level (Flahive & Snow, 1980: analysis 2; Perkins, 1980), nor did it prove to be one of the measures that emerged on a discriminant analysis of three program levels (Flahive & Snow, 1980: analysis 1). However, the score did progress from 1.17 to 1.33 to 1.39 to 1.35 to 1.40 to 1.47 across six levels (although they were collapsed to three levels for the discriminant analysis). The usefulness of such a weighted index is not clear. It does seem promising to assign values to the structures that actually appear in advanced learners' writing as a way to measure language development, although a detailed analysis of the development of the individual structures would be necessary first.

CONCLUSION: GRAMMATICAL COMPLEXITY MEASURES

Clauses appear to be an important component of language development. The T-unit complexity ratio (clauses per T-unit, or C/T) generally increased in a linear relationship to proficiency level across studies, regardless of task, target language, significance, or how proficiency was defined. Just as for the best fluency measures, there was more likely to be a significant relationship between T-unit complexity and proficiency when proficiency level was defined as a program or school level than as short-term change or judgments made about writing done within intact classes. Two other measures of clause depth, the number of dependent clauses per total clauses (DC/C) or T-units (DC/T) also increased linearly with respect to proficiency level, and the DC/C measure was significantly related to program level. However, for the coordination measure of the number of T-units per sentence (T/S), which should decline with proficiency, there were mixed results. The relationship between these measures and proficiency level and holistic ratings is shown in Table 14 below, with inconsistent ratios indicated in bold type.

Table 14: Comparison of means on complexity measures across studies that examine multiple programs or school levels

Timed essay, proficiency = program or school level			
study/levels	C/T	DC/C	T/S
Cooper, 1976			
sophomores	1.2		1.2
juniors	1.4		1.2
seniors	1.5		1.2
graduates	1.4		1.2
natives	1.7		1.3
Flahive & Snow, 1980			
level 1	**1.07**		
level 2	1.28		
level 3	1.56		
level 4	1.92		
level 5	1.92		
level 6	1.74		
Hirano, 1991			
low	1.23	.18	
mid	1.35	.25	
high	1.52	.33	

| Rewriting task, proficiency = program or school level | | | |
study/levels	C/T	DC/C	T/S
Monroe, 1976			
freshmen	1.20		1.37
sophomores	1.45		1.28
juniors/seniors	1.51		1.24
graduates	1.51		1.24
natives	1.64		1.10
Sharma, 1980			
low intermediate	1.33		
high intermediate	1.39		
advanced	1.45		

| Timed essay, proficiency = holistic rating of range of levels | | | |
study/levels	C/T	DC/C	T/S
Homburg, 1984			
rating 5	.38		1.35
rating 6	.54		1.59
rating 7	.60		1.37
Kameen, 1979			
'poor'	1.66	.37	
'good'	1.74	.40	

Based on these studies, measures of the depth of clauses (C/T) and clause types (DC/C, DC/T) appear to have construct validity as measures of complexity in language development because they exhibit a linear relationship to proficiency level across studies that used a wide range of levels. Various other successful grammatical complexity measures also suggest that passives, articles, relative clauses, and complex nominals may be important structures relative to developmental level.

CHAPTER FIVE

THE LEXICAL COMPLEXITY MEASURES

The richness of a writer's lexicon constitutes another major area in which complexity can be measured, since "the possession of a reasonably large lexicon" is crucial for effective communication (Hyltenstam, 1988, p. 71). Lexical complexity is manifest in writing primarily in terms of the range (lexical variation) and size (lexical sophistication) of a second language writer's productive vocabulary. Lexical complexity means that a wide variety of basic and sophisticated words are available and can be accessed quickly, whereas a lack of complexity means that only a narrow range of basic words are available or can be accessed. An analysis of lexical complexity is not concerned with how many words are present in the writing, but with how varied or sophisticated the words or word types are. Learners who have more productive vocabulary items available to them are able to vary their word choices more freely; consequently, larger ratios on variation and sophistication measures should reveal greater lexical proficiency. Memory for chunks may also be related to vocabulary learning (Ellis, 1996).

Measures of fluency, accuracy, and complexity in second language development can all relate to the lexicon. We have already considered lexical fluency measures such as the number of words (W) or verbs (V) that occur in a composition. These frequency counts measure quantity, not variation or sophistication, so they are considered fluency measures rather than complexity measures. We have already considered lexical accuracy measures such as the number of lexical errors per clause (LexE/C), verb lexical errors per verb (VLexE/V), and lexical errors per lexical word (LexE/LW), as well as several accuracy indices related to the lexicon, including a lexical quality index and a lexical accuracy index. The ratio measures focused on accuracy, but the two indices included features of both accuracy and complexity.

In this section, we are going to examine the lexical measures that relate to complexity, the majority of which are ratio measures. Only Harley and King (1989) used a frequency measure, counting the number of verb types (VT) in written samples, while there have been no indices that examine lexical complexity exclusively. As for the ratio measures, although most researchers refer to 'type/token' ratios as if they were the only type of lexical measure, there are actually three types of ratio measures that have been used to measure lexical complexity: type/token ratios such as the ratio of word types to total words (WT/W), type/type ratios such as the ratio of sophisticated word types to total number of word types (SWT/WT), and token/token ratios such as the ratio of lexical words to overall words (LW/W). Furthermore, these three ratio types have been used to measure variation, density, and sophistication, as the following chart shows:

variation	type/token	word types per words
		verb types per verbs
		lexical word types per lexical words
density	token/token	lexical words per words
sophistication	type/token	sophisticated verb types per verbs
	type/type	sophisticated word types per word types
		basic word types per word types
	token/token	sophisticated lexical words per lexical words
		individual lexical words per lexical words

The lexical variation measures have all been type/token ratios, including a word type per total words measure (WT/W), a verb type per total verbs measure (VT/V), and a lexical word type per total lexical words measure (LWT/LW). There has only been one measure of density, a token/token ratio of proportion of lexical words to total words (LW/W). But the lexical sophistication measures have included all three measure types: 1) a type/token ratio of sophisticated verb types to total verbs (SVT/V), 2) type/type ratios of sophisticated word types to total word types (SWT/WT) and basic word types to total word types (BWT/WT), and 3) token/token ratios of sophisticated lexical words to total lexical words (SLW/LW) and individual lexical words to total lexical words (ILW/LW).

Type/token ratios (but not the other two types) have been criticized because they are sensitive to text length. There is a negative relationship between a type/token ratio and sample size, with the ratio decreasing as sample size increases and more of the words reoccur (Carroll, 1967). This has caused some researchers to take equivalent samples from each writer, limited to the length of the smallest sample (e.g., Arnaud, 1992). Length sizes of these samples have varied, although Hess, Sefton, and Landry (1986) view 350 tokens as the minimally reliable sample to conduct a comparison based on the oral speech of preschool children. The assumption behind limiting the sample size is that if someone is given the opportunity to produce a larger sample, his type/token ratio score will be proportionately lower.

There is a different way in which type/token ratios are not appropriately sensitive to length, however. When a sample is collected under timed conditions, if one learner produces a longer sample with a certain proportion of word types, but another learner produces a shorter sample with the same proportion of word types (hence fewer overall types), they would both receive exactly the same type/token ratio score. This isn't desirable, because the one who maintained the proportion over a larger number of words in the same amount of time clearly exhibits greater lexical complexity. Consequently, some researchers have attempted to calculate the type/token ratio in a manner that attempts to take length into account in a more appropriate way. For example, Arthur (1979) calculated the number of word types divided by the square root of two times the total number of words (WT/√2W) based on Carroll (1967), and Chaudron and Parker (1990) calculated the number of verb types squared divided by the number of verbs (VT2/V). For these two measures, as both length and number of types increases, the score increases.

These types of alternatives are criticized by Hess et al. (1986) because they are not completely independent of sample size. However, in comparisons of second language learners when there are time or conceptual limits, we feel that a measure that increases as length and number of types increases is a better measure. In Chaudron and Parker (1990), the oral sample used for measuring the verb type/token ratio was conceptually limited by the picture description task, and in Arthur (1979), the written sample was limited by the amount of time allotted to the writers. In both of these studies, a longer sample with many word types got a higher score than either a shorter sample with many types or a longer sample with fewer types, which is a desirable result. We don't think that type/token ratios should be used unless there is either a time limit or a conceptual limit on production, and one of the two alternative ways to calculate the ratio is used.

LEXICAL COMPLEXITY FREQUENCIES

Almost no research has been done using frequency measures of lexical complexity, as indicated by the lack of studies in Table 15. The only exception is Harley and King (1989), who compared bilingual and second language sixth-grade students on number of verb types (VT) in their narratives and letters. Unsurprisingly, they found a significant difference on this measure, indicating that native writers have more verbs available in their lexical repertoire. Since ratio measures are more valid than frequency measures, there is no need for further research in this domain.

Table 15. Lexical complexity frequencies: Number of studies by type of result

measure	code	***	**	*	X
verb type	VT		1		

*** Developmental measures that highly correlate with proficiency (r=.65+), or show an overall effect for proficiency (p<.05) together with a significant difference between three or more adjacent proficiency levels (p<.05).

** Developmental measures that moderately correlate with proficiency (r=.45–.64), or show an overall effect for proficiency for two or more proficiency levels (p<.05).

* Developmental measures that weakly correlate with proficiency (r=.25–.44), or show a trend towards an effect for proficiency (p<.10).

X Developmental measures that show no correlation with or effect for proficiency.

Verb type (VT)

VT = number of verb types	
***	
**	Harley & King 89
*	
X	

Harley and King (1989) compared bilingual and second language sixth-grade students on the number of verb types (VT) in their narratives and letters. They found a significant difference between the two groups, with the native speakers producing more verb types than the second language students, presumably because they had more verbs available to access and were able to produce more writing overall.

LEXICAL COMPLEXITY RATIOS

Several types of ratio measures have been utilized in research on second language lexical development in writing. These include type/token ratios such as a measure of word variation used by Cumming and Mellow (1996) that calculates the ratio of word types to total words (WT/W), type/type ratios such as a lexical sophistication measure used by Laufer (1994) that calculates the ratio of sophisticated word types to overall number of word types (SWT/WT), and token/token ratios such as a lexical density measure used by Linnarud (1986) that calculates the ratio of lexical words to overall words (LW/W). The purpose of these types of measures is to determine the lexical characteristics of more proficient writers. Several of these studies also used lexical co^{mplexity} measures in comparisons between second language writers and native speakers (Harley & King, 1989; Hyltenstam, 1988; Linnarud, 1986; McClure, 1991).

Table 16 shows the results for the various lexical complexity ratios that have been used in studies of second language development. As can be seen in the table, each measure has been used in only a few studies although the results are quite good with respect to significance. It appears that variation and sophistication, but not density, are related to language development. With respect to variation, the most notable result was for a word variation measure that takes into account both the length and number of types of the written text (WT$^{/\sqrt{2}W}$, in Arthur, 1979: study 1). This measure was able to capture changes in word variation from the first half of a writing class to the second. In addition, a lexical variation measure (the ratio of lexical word types to lexical words; LWT/LW) significantly correlated with holistic ratings in Engber's (1995) study of intermediate and advanced proficiency levels, while the variation measures noun types per lexical words (NT/LW) and modifier types per lexical words (ModT/LW) examined by McClure significantly differentiated between bilingual and monolingual school children. With respect to sophistication, Laufer's (1994) study of various measures of lexical sophistication and basicness showed that measures at the 2000-word frequency level significantly differentiated essays written 14 and 28 weeks apart for two groups of advanced learners. And Harley and King (1992) found a significant difference in the ratio of sophisticated verb types to total verbs (SVT/V) between sixth grade native and second language students. Apparently, lexical sophistication measures do relate to differences in language proficiency.

However, the lexical density measure of lexical words per total words (LW/W) doesn't appear to be related to proficiency. It doesn't differentiate natives from second language speakers (Linnarud, 1986: analysis 1; Hyltenstam, 1988), nor proficiency levels (Linnarud, 1986: analysis 2; Nihalani, 1981; Engber, 1995), presumably because the proportion of lexical words to total words seems to be fairly constant across samples. Apparently, density is dependent on the grammatical system of the language, which dictates how many high-frequency grammatical words must be used in proportion to lexical words.

Table 16. Lexical complexity ratios: Number of studies by type of result

measure	code	***	**	*	X
word variation–1	WT/W			1	2
word variation–2	WT/√2W	1			1
verb variation–1	VT/V	1			
verb sophistication	SVT/V	1			
lexical variation	LWT/LW		2		6
noun variation	NT/LW	1			
verb variation–2	VT/LW				1
adjective variation	AdjT/LW		1		
adverb variation	AdvT/LW	1			
modifier variation	ModT/LW	1			
lexical density	LW/W			1	4
lexical individuality	ILW/LW		1	1	

continued...

Table 16. Lexical complexity ratios: Number of studies by type of result (cont.)

measure	code	***	**	*	X
lexical sophistication–1	SLW/LW	1	2		
lexical sophistication–2	SWT/WT	4		2	
lexical basicness	BWT/WT	2	1	1	

*** Developmental measures that highly correlate with proficiency (r=.65+), or show an overall effect for proficiency (p<.05) together with a significant difference between three or more adjacent proficiency levels (p<.05).

** Developmental measures that moderately correlate with proficiency (r=.45–.64), or show an overall effect for proficiency for two or more proficiency levels (p<.05).

* Developmental measures that weakly correlate with proficiency (r=.25–.44), or show a trend towards an effect for proficiency (p<.10).

X Developmental measures that show no correlation with or effect for proficiency.

Word variation–1 (WT/W)

WT/W = total number of different word types divided by total number of words (word tokens)

***	
**	
*	McClure 91
X	Cumming & Mellow 96: analysis 1, analysis 2

One type/token ratio used to measure how varied words are is a ratio of the number of word types to number of total words (WT/W). Cumming and Mellow (1996) investigated this measure with Japanese and French learners of English who were at intermediate and advanced levels of English proficiency, but found no significant relationship between placements and word variation, although the means differed in the expected direction. In the French group, the intermediate learners had a 47.3 word types per word score while the advanced learners had 48.3. In the Japanese group, the intermediate learners had a 48.9 word types per word score while the advanced learners had 51.2. McClure (1991) compared the word variation of Spanish-English bilinguals and English monolinguals, finding a trend, although the report of the means doesn't reveal a particular direction (word variation ratios varied from .26 to .44 for different sample lengths).

Neither McClure nor Cumming and Mellow limited the length of the samples used, despite well-known criticisms of this measure (Carroll, 1967; Arnaud, 1992; Hess et al., 1986). The two problems with this type/token measure is that it doesn't discriminate between a writer who uses a few types in a short composition and a writer who uses more types in a longer composition, and it doesn't react appropriately to length of the sample; the score gets lower as a composition gets longer because the types repeat more often.

Word variation–2 (WT/√2W)
WT/√2W = total number of different word types divided by the square root of
two times the total number of words (word tokens)

***	
**	Arthur 79: study 1
*	
X	Arthur 79: study 2

Another type/token ratio used to measure how varied words are is a ratio of the number of word types to the square root of two times the word tokens (WT/√2W), a measure developed by Carroll (1967). This measure factors into the ratio the number of words written, since the use of more types in a longer text counts more than the same proportion of types in a shorter text. The score on this type/token measure increases as the length or number of types increases. Using this measure, Arthur (1979: study 1) found a significant difference in word variation between the first four weeks of class (4.31 WT/√2W) and the second four weeks (4.47 WT/√2W) in timed compositions written by a low-intermediate writing class. However, the same measure did not differentiate holistic rankings of the compositions (study two). This measure attempts to solve the problems noted for the previous word variation measure because it rewards the presence of many types in a longer composition, despite the increased repetition of those types.

Consider the comparison in Table 17 between six hypothetical writing samples written under the same time constraint, analyzed with three possible word variation measures: words types per words (WT/W), word types per square root of two times the words (WT/√2W; Carroll, 1967), and word types squared per total words (WT2/W; adapted from Chaudron & Parker, 1990).

Table 17. Comparison of type/token formulas

	word types	words	WT/W	WT/√2W	WT^2/W
A	20	100	.05	1.41	4.00
B	25	100	.25	1.77	6.25
C	10	40	.25	1.12	2.50
D	20	80	.25	1.58	5.00
E	10	20	.50	1.58	5.00
F	20	40	.50	2.24	10.00

The WT/W measure ranks the samples in order from writer A, with the lowest variation, to writers E and F, with the highest variation. The WT/W measure ignores length when type/token ratios of the same proportion are compared (check B versus C versus D and E versus F), but is also severely negatively affected by length when the same number of types are produced in a much longer sample (check A versus D versus F). Clearly, this is a misguided result, because it fails t° ^{ca}pture the fact that the two writers that show the most word variation are B and F, B with the most types and largest number of words, and F with slightly fewer types but a higher proportion of types to tokens than B.

The other two alternative measures work much better and rank the writers in exactly the same order (from C to A to D/E to B to F), so they can be seen as numerically equivalent variants of each other. Using these latter two measures, a writer with the same proportion of types to tokens but many more words gets a higher ranking (compare A to C and F to E), but still the proportion of types to tokens counts more than purely the number of types (hence F receiving a higher score than B, and E receiving the same score as D). These may not be perfect measures, but they are superior to the WT/W alternative, and do allow the incorporation of length differences under timed conditions.

Verb variation–1 (VT/V)

VT/V = total number of different verb types divided by total number of verbs (tokens)

***	
**	Harley & King 89
*	
X	

Harley and King (1989) compared native and second language sixth-grade students on the ratio of verb types to verb tokens (VT/T) in their narratives and letters. They found that French immersion second language writers used significantly fewer types of verbs (0.43) than the native language writers (0.54) on timed-writing tasks. Since they didn't limit the sample size, a better measure would be the one developed by Chaudron and Parker (1989) VT2/V, or an adaptation of the measure developed by Carroll (1964) to VT/$\sqrt{2V}$.

Verb sophistication (SVT/V)

SVT/V = total number of sophisticated (infrequent) verb types divided by **total number of verbs**

***	
**	Harley & King 89: SVT–1 and SVT–2
*	
X	

Harley and King (1989) also investigated two type/token ratios of sophisticated verb types to total verbs (SVT/V) for sixth grade native and second language students. On one measure, they counted sophisticated verbs as those that don't appear on a frequency list of the 20 most frequent French verbs, while on the other measure, they counted sophisticated verbs as those that don't appear in a frequency list of approximately 200 French verbs. For both sets of criteria, they found that the native language writers used significantly more sophisticated verbs than the second language immersion writers. Based on the 20 word frequency list, the learners had a .29 sophisticated verb types per verb average, while the native speakers had a .40 average. Based on the 200 word frequency list, the learners had a .08 sophisticated verb types per verb average, while the native speakers had a .17 average. Since they didn't limit the sample size, a better measure would be the one developed by Chaudron and Parker (1989) SVT^2/V, or an adaptation of the measure developed by Carroll (1964) to $SVT/\sqrt{2V}$.

Lexical variation (LWT/LW)

LWT/LW = total number of different lexical word types divided by total number of lexical words

***	
**	Engber 95; Linnarud 86: analysis 1
*	
X	Casanave 94; Hyltenstam 88; Laufer 94: analysis 1, analysis 2; Linnarud 86: analysis 2; Nihalani 81

Lexical variation is a type/token measure that examines the ratio of different lexical word types to total number of lexical word tokens (LWT/LW). This measure captures the intuition that second language writers at a higher proficiency level will command a larger vocabulary and will be able to use significantly more lexical word types than writers at a lower proficiency level. This is supported in Engber (1995), who found a significant relationship between holistic ratings and lexical variation for learners at intermediate and advanced levels, and Linnarud (1986: analysis 1), who found a significant difference between native and second language writers on this measure. However, Laufer (1994) found no effect for instruction with advanced learners on this measure, Hyltenstam (1988) found no difference between native and near-native writers, and Linnarud (1986) and Nihalani (1981) found no relationship between holistic scores and this measure for groups at the same school level. Casanave (1994), in an analysis of lexical word types per lexical word in the journal entries of five intermediate learners over three semesters, found relatively consistent percentages of lexical word types per lexical word for each learner across entries. Only Engber's (1995) study applied this measure to learners at a range of proficiency levels, and her study was significant.

A comparison of the studies shows that in Laufer (1994), the means on lexical word types per lexical word ranged from .43 to .46, whereas in Casanave (1994), Linnarud (1986), Nihalani (1981), and Hyltenstam (1988) the means on lexical word types per lexical word ranged from .51 to .84. Considering the relatively advanced proficiency levels of all of these writers, this discrepancy doesn't make sense, unless the criteria for inclusion as a type was different, such as a discrepancy with word classes like prepositions. However, none of these researchers explicitly defined lexical words.

Linnarud (1986: analysis 2) attributed the absence of a correlation to the differing length of the writings, because lexical variation decreases as the number of words in a text increases. However, when Hyltenstam (1988) calculated lexical variation controlling for length, he still found no significant difference. In fact, his subjects were near-native writers of English, and in the majority of studies using this measure the learners were advanced. As noted above, the range of scores was quite similar in all the studies that reported means except for Laufer (1994). While it is possible that this measure may work better with lower proficiency learners, some caution is needed because it is possible that high lexical variation can result from poor text construction, if there is a lack of coherence in the writing that will prevent the same content words from appearing repeatedly (Hyltenstam, 1988). It also might improve the results if the alternative formula LWT/√2LW were used.

Noun variation (NT/LW)

NT/LW = total number of different noun types divided by total number of lexical words

***	
**	McClure 91
*	
X	

McClure (1991) compared Spanish-English bilingual and English monolingual 4th and 9th grade school children on a variety of lexical word variation type/token measures. The first of these was a measure of noun variation, or the number of different noun types divided by the total number of lexical words (NT/LW). She found that the monolinguals had a significantly lower noun variation ratio than the bilinguals (.32 versus .39 respectively), indicating that the bilinguals were relying on proportionately more nouns in their writing. The length of the samples was not controlled.

Verb variation–2 (VT/LW)

VT/LW = total number of different verb types divided by total number of lexical words

***	
**	
*	
X	McClure 91

McClure (1991) also compared Spanish-English bilingual and English monolingual 4th and 9th grade school children on a type/token measure of verb variation, or the number of different verb types divided by the total number of lexical words (VT/LW). This is a variant of the verb variation type/token ratio used by Harley and King (1989), which was the number of verb types divided by the number of verbs (VT/V). McClure found no difference between the monolingual and bilingual groups, with the means at .35 for both groups. The length of the samples was not controlled.

Adjective variation (AdjT/LW)

AdjT/LW = total number of different adjective types divided by total number of lexical words

***	
**	
*	McClure 91
X	

McClure (1991) also compared Spanish-English bilingual and English monolingual 4th and 9th grade school children on a type/token measure of adjective variation, or the number of different adjective types divided by the total number of lexical words (AdjT/LW). She found that the monolinguals had a slightly higher adjective variation ratio than the bilinguals (.17 versus .16 respectively), with a trend towards significance (p=.10), indicating that the monolinguals were relying on proportionately more adjectives in their writing. The length of the samples was not controlled.

Adverb variation (AdvT/LW)

AdvT/LW = total number of different adverb types divided by total number of lexical words

***	
**	McClure 91
*	
X	

McClure (1991) also compared Spanish-English bilingual and English monolingual 4th and 9th grade school children on a type/token measure of adverb variation, or the number of different adverb types divided by the total number of lexical words (AdvT/LW). She found that the monolinguals had a significantly higher adverb variation ratio than the bilinguals (.16 versus .13 respectively), indicating that the monolinguals were relying on proportionately more adverbs in their writing. The length of the samples was not controlled.

Modifier variation (ModT/LW)

ModT/LW = total number of different modifier types divided by total number of lexical words

***	
**	McClure 91
*	
X	

McClure (1991) also compared Spanish-English bilingual and English monolingual 4th and 9th grade school children on a type/token measure of modifier variation, or the number of adverb and adjective types divided by the total number of lexical words (ModT/LW). She found that the monolinguals had a significantly higher modifier variation ratio than the bilinguals (.33 versus .29 respectively), indicating that the monolinguals were relying on proportionately more modifiers in their writing. The length of the samples was not controlled.

Lexical density (LW/W)

LW/W = total number of lexical words divided by total number of words

***	
**	
*	Linnarud 86: analysis 1
X	Engber 95; Hyltenstam 88; Linnarud 86: analysis 2; Nihalani 81

Lexical density is a measure of the proportion of lexical words to total words (LW/W). This is a token/token ratio. Lexical words are all open-class words, rather than closed-class grammatical words such as prepositions, determiners, or auxiliaries. It is not obvious to us what developmental prediction is expected for lexical density, although the assumption seems to be that a higher score would indicate greater language development. Rather, we feel that beginning learners might use fewer grammatical words than higher level learners or native speakers, resulting in a higher ratio for the lowest developmental levels, but little difference at higher levels. However, in Linnarud (1986: analysis 1), native language writers had a slightly higher lexical density figure (.44) than second language writers (.42) though the difference was only a trend towards significance (p<0.07). In fact, the figures were slightly higher than what was observed to be one native speaker norm of .40 in Ure (1971). Nor did Hyltenstam (1988) find any significant difference in lexical density between near-native writers (.45 and .44) and native writers (.45). Furthermore, none of the studies that compared holistic ratings of writing with the lexical density measure found any significant result (Linnarud, 1986: analysis 2; Nihalani, 1981; Engber, 1995). The results for Nihalani ranged from .46 to .47, but the others didn't report the means. Hyltenstam (1988) acknowledges that lexical density may not be the best measure of language development because it's possible to get a high density score with a small vocabulary, or if more lexical items rather than anaphoric devices such as lexical repetition are used. Nihalani (1981) used a take-home composition for her analysis, which might have affected the results as well.

Lexical individuality (ILW/LW)

ILW/LW = total number of lexical words unique to the writer divided by total number of lexical words

***	
**	Linnarud 86: analysis 2
*	Linnarud 86: analysis 1
X	

Linnarud (1986), having noticed that native language writers used many more original words than second language writers, thought that a measure that determined how many words were unique to an second language writer might indicate the level of lexical development. In order to calculate lexical individuality, it's necessary to determine which words are unique to a single writer among the entire group. Then the number of words individual to each writer is divided by that writers' total lexical words (ILW/LW). This is a token/token ratio. She then investigated the correlation between lexical individuality and holistic ratings of picture descriptions, and found it to be significant (analysis 2), but didn't report the means, although they appear to range between .10 and .28 based on a graph. She also compared the lexical individuality of the learners (.13) to native speakers (.23) but didn't do a statistical test of the difference (analysis 1). The utility of the measure as index of second language lexical development is doubtful, however, not only because originality of word choice might not be a valid concept for language development, but also that uniqueness varies with the particular corpus.

Lexical sophistication–1 (SLW/LW)

SLW/LW = total number of sophisticated lexical words divided by total number of lexical words

***	
**	Linnarud 86: analysis 1
*	Hyltenstam 88; Linnarud 86: analysis 2
X	

Unlike lexical individuality, the concept of a measure of lexical sophistication is intuitively appealing as an indicator of lexical development. Lexical sophistication is measured by determining which lexical words in a written sample are not on a list of basic words, or are on a list of sophisticated words, as a percentage of the total lexical words (SLW/LW). This is a token/token ratio. Linnarud (1986: analysis 1, analysis 2) defined sophisticated lexical words as those English words that are generally introduced at grade 9 and above in the Swedish educational system, and found that native language writers used significantly more sophisticated vocabulary than second language writers (.25 versus .12), but found only a small correlation between the ratio of sophisticated words and holistic ratings of the writing samples. Hyltenstam (1988) defined sophisticated lexical words as words that were not included among the 7,000 most frequent Swedish words, but he found no significant difference between the native speakers (.16) and either second language group (.16 and .13).

Lexical sophistication–2 (SWT/WT)

SWT/WT = total number of sophisticated word types divided by total number of word types

***	
**	Laufer 94: analysis 1 (university word list, 2000+), analysis 2 (university word list, 2000+)
*	
X	Laufer 94: analysis 1 (1000+, other), analysis 2 (1000+, other)

Another measure of lexical sophistication used by Laufer (1994) is the calculation of the total number of sophisticated word types divided by the total number of word types (SWT/WT). This is a type/type ratio. She did not restrict her count to lexical words, but counted all types of words. Laufer analyzed four different measures of sophistication on pre-and post-compositions written by two advanced university classes. In two of the analyses, she counted sophisticated words as words not on a 2000-word frequency list and words on a university-level word list, and found the measures significant for both groups. In the other two analyses, she counted sophisticated words as words not on a 1000-word frequency list, and words not on any of her frequency lists, and found no significant effect. This suggests that although the lexical sophistication measure appears to point to lexical development in writing, it may depend on how the sophisticated words are defined. The means for these measures ranged from .04 to .13 depending on the group and how sophistication was defined.

Lexical basicness (BWT/WT)

BWT/WT = total number of basic word types divided by total number of word types

***	
**	Laufer 94: analysis 1 (2000), analysis 2 (2000)
*	Laufer 94: analysis 1 (1000)
X	Laufer 94: analysis 2 (1000)

Laufer (1994) also developed a type/type measure related to lexical sophistication that essentially measures lexical basicness, or how many basic word types per total word types (BWT/WT) are used. She used two measures of basicness: words on a 1000-word frequency list, and words on a 2000-word frequency list. In her analysis of compositions written by two advanced university classes either 14 weeks (analysis 1) or 28 weeks (analysis 2) apart, she found that the measure of lexical basicness using the 2000-word list significantly differentiated both groups on their pre- and post-compositions. However, the 1000-word list did not differentiate the groups significantly, although it approached a trend for one of them. The means for these measures ranged from .82 to .92 depending on the group and how basicness was defined.

CONCLUSION: LEXICAL COMPLEXITY MEASURES

Measures of lexical variation and sophistication, but not lexical density, appear to be related to second language development, although the number of studies of lexical complexity are few and have tended to compare native with second language speakers rather than developmental with proficiency measures. These studies showed that a word type variation measure that takes length into account (WT/$\sqrt{2W}$) significantly increased by the end of a course (from 4.31 for the first six compositions to 4.47 for the last six compositions, in Arthur, 1979). A sophisticated word type ratio (SWT/WT) also significantly increased after one or two semesters of instruction, although significance depended on the actual word list used. For university students, a sophistication ratio based on a 2000-word list and a university word list were significant for two groups, but a sophistication ratio based on a 1000-word list was not. Based on the 2000-word list, one group increased from 9.96 to 13.17 SWT/WT after one semester of instruction, while another group increased from 8.48 to 10.04 after two semesters of instruction (in Laufer, 1994). Although these two lexical complexity variation and sophistication measures haven't been systematically investigated in many studies or for many program levels, they do offer promise as indicators of language development.

CHAPTER SIX

THE BEST DEVELOPMENTAL MEASURES

We have examined more than one hundred measures of language development that were used in studies of second language writing to measure fluency, accuracy, grammatical complexity, and lexical complexity. Of these measures, which are the best indicators of developmental level? Does second language use in writing develop fluency, accuracy, and complexity in a linear progression?

We have defined *fluency* as the rapid production of language, *accuracy* as error-free production, and *complexity* as the use of varied and sophisticated structures and vocabulary. When we measure fluency, we are measuring the observable outcome of automaticity of access, and when we measure accuracy or complexity, we are measuring the observable outcome of representation and restructuring. We agree with Ellis (1996) that the representation of language, the restructuring of that representation, and the development of automatic access to the developing representation may all arise from a single learning process: the gradual strengthening of memories for language chunks. We are measuring the fluency, accuracy, and complexity of language use in order to view the effects of that learning process, and we want to consider which measures have proved the most revealing.

CRITERIA FOR JUDGING THE BEST DEVELOPMENTAL MEASURES

Although there are different possible criteria for judging which developmental measures are the most useful, we decided to do a meta-analysis of the reliability and validity of the measures in their relationship to proficiency level across studies. The studies that have examined fluency, accuracy, and complexity in second language writing have varied greatly in which developmental measures they have employed and in how they have determined proficiency levels. The variety of ways that proficiency has been conceptualized include rating scales, standardized tests, program levels, school levels, classroom grades, short-term change in intact classes, and comparisons with native speakers. This variability makes direct comparisons between measures or studies difficult, so we were forced to look at larger issues in determining which developmental measures are the most successful.

In evaluating each developmental measure, we wanted to find support for the construct validity of that measure across studies. First, we were looking for repeated sampling reliability, which would be the consistency of the measure with different subjects. The evidence would be a consistent, linear progression of the measure according to externally-determined proficiency levels across different studies. This means that regardless of how proficiency levels were defined in a study, each level would have to show an increase in its average score on the measure. Second, we were looking for concurrent validity in particular contexts, which would be a consistently statistically significant or highly-correlated relationship between the developmental measure and either program or school levels. These proved to be more reliable contexts for judging developmental differences than holistic ratings, grades, standardized test scores, short-term change, or native-speaker comparisons. Although language development is not the same as proficiency level, measures of language development ought to be able to distinguish between learners at clearly different levels of proficiency. We felt that any measures that met both of these criteria — having both repeated sampling reliability across studies and concurrent validity in particular contexts — would be measures of second language development that exhibited a certain degree of construct validity.

A better criteria for evaluating the construct validity of developmental measures of fluency, accuracy, and complexity might be to determine whether they are related to known developmental sequences such as stages of negation, question-formation, relative-clause formation, or morpheme acquisition. Because this has not been done, we were unable to use this as a criteria, but we see this as an area for potentially fruitful future research.

THE BEST FLUENCY, ACCURACY, AND COMPLEXITY MEASURES SO FAR

We found that there was a difference between the accuracy measures and the fluency and complexity measures in how they related to external proficiency measures. The accuracy measures were most often significantly related to holistic judgments, and were consistently linear for holistic judgments and short-term change in intact classes, whereas the fluency and complexity measures were most often significantly related to program or school levels, and were consistently linear across a range of program, school, or holistic levels.

These results suggest that fluency and complexity measures may be related to the construct 'development,' but that accuracy measures may be related to a different construct 'error.' In fact, in discussions of potential trade-offs in the developmental literature, researchers have indicated that there may be trade-offs between accuracy and complexity (Foster & Skehan, 1996; Tedick, 1990) or accuracy and fluency (Hamp-Lyons, 1991; MacKay, 1982), but there has been no mention of a potential trade-off between fluency and complexity. If fluency and complexity measures do prove to be inter-related, it would support our theoretical claim that the same learning process (increasingly strengthened memories for language instances or chunks) is behind both automaticity (which leads to fluency) and restructuring (which leads to complexity). This would be an important area to investigate by means of a principal components analysis or factor analysis.

The fluency measures that were consistently linear and significantly related to program or school levels were words per T-unit (W/T), words per clause (W/C) and words per error-free T-unit (W/EFT). The grammatical complexity measures that were consistently linear and significantly related to program or school levels were clauses per T-unit (C/T) and dependent clauses per clause (DC/C). In addition, two lexical complexity measures that were significantly related to short-term change were a word type measure (WT/√2W) and a sophisticated word type measure (SWT/WT), but these measures were not investigated across program levels.

The accuracy measures that were significantly related to short-term change and holistic judgments across a range of levels and within intact classes were error-free T-units per T-unit (EFT/T) and errors per T-unit (E/T). These measures were only consistently linear in these contexts, but not across program or school levels. Although the measure error-free T-units (EFT) was also important, because it is a frequency measure rather than a ratio measure, it is far less useful for comparisons across studies. The best measures are summarized in the chart below.

best measures of 'development' so far	
fluency	W/T, W/C, W/EFT
grammatical complexity	C/T, DC/C
lexical complexity	WT/√2W, SWT/WT
best measures of 'error' so far	
accuracy	EFT/T, E/T

Unfortunately, almost no studies have compared all four types of measures for one population of learners, except for Casanave (1994), who created individual profiles based on W/T, W/EFT, EFT/T, C/T, and LWT/LW, among other measures. However, she did not compare proficiency levels, report overall means, or do any statistical tests on these measures, so a comparison between them isn't possible. Only a few studies investigated the three most common types of measures (fluency, accuracy, and grammatical complexity), and of these, only three (Homburg, 1984; Flahive & Snow, 1980; Vann, 1979) did a statistical comparison among the measures, as the next section will show.

THE RELATIONSHIP BETWEEN TYPES OF DEVELOPMENTAL MEASURES

All but one of the studies that have investigated developmental measures related them to some external measure of proficiency (only Mendelsohn, 1983, did not), but very few of them investigated the relationship among the developmental measures themselves. Only three studies have examined correlations between measures (Mendelsohn, 1983; Laufer, 1994; Yau, 1991). In developmental measure studies, correlations would reveal the strength of the relationship between pairs of developmental measures.

Mendelsohn (1983) did a rank-order correlation between scores on T-unit length (W/T) and syntactic accuracy (SynE/W) and found a low correlation of r=.31. He claimed that a low correlation shows that both types of measures are necessary for describing language use, because they capture different aspects of development. This is consistent with our distinction between words per T-unit (W/T) as a fluency measure and a variety of accuracy measures.

Yau (1991) found strong correlations among the four fluency measures that she investigated (W/T, W/C, WCN/T, WCN/C), with the strongest correlation between words in complex nominals per T-unit and words in complex nominals per clause (r=.91). She found a somewhat weaker relationship between T-unit length and clause length (r=.68). She found a strong correlation between T-unit length (W/T) and words in complex nominals per T-unit (r=.82), suggesting that one major source of length in T-units is complexity of the nominals. She found a similarly strong correlation between clause length (W/C) and words in complex nominals per clause (r=.77). Of even more interest is the developmental differences in correlations, as the following chart shows.

	ESL grade 9	ESL grade 13
WCN/T and WCN/C	.91	.89
W/T and W/C	.80	.54
W/T and WCN/T	.48	.77
W/C and WCN/C	.19	.76

This shows that at both stages of language development, the number of complex nominals in T-units and clauses is highly correlated but that the number of words in T-units and clauses is not, except for the lower level group (ESL grade 9). For this group, clause length was only slightly shorter than T-unit length (7.62 W/C versus 10.82 W/T), presumably because the majority of T-units had only one clause in them. For the older group, T-units were much longer than clauses (10.48 W/C versus 15.54 W/T). Furthermore, the relationship between complex nominals and length for both T-units and clauses is stronger at the higher proficiency level, suggesting that nominals become a major source of T-unit or clause length as language develops. This shows how revealing a correlation analysis among measures at different proficiency levels can be.

Laufer (1994) found no correlation between a measure of lexical sophistication (sophisticated word types per total word types; SWT/WT) and a measure of lexical variation (lexical word types per total lexical words; LWT/LW). The lack of a correlation was because the sophistication measure related to change over time while the variation measure did not. Laufer claimed that lexical variation doesn't measure how large the lexicon is, only how varied it is for that particular individual, but that lexical sophistication does measure the size of the lexicon against an external standard (the frequency of sophisticated words).

Another type of analysis that compares measures is a discriminant analysis, which is the inverse of an analysis of variance. For developmental studies, a discriminant analysis would identify which developmental measures are the best predictors of membership in distinct groups based on proficiency level. However, only four studies have examined which measures are the best discriminators among measures of proficiency (Arthur, 1979; Flahive & Snow, 1980; Homburg, 1984; Vann, 1979).

Homburg (1984), in a discriminant analysis relating developmental measures to three adjacent levels of a holistic rating scale, found that five measures together accounted for 84% of the variance among the levels. They were second-degree errors per T-unit (2DE/T), the number of dependent clauses (DC), the number of words per sentence (W/S), the number of coordinating connectors (CConn), and the number of error-free T-units (EFT). These include one fluency, two accuracy, and two complexity measures. The most notable of the measures that did not emerge as discriminators were words per T-unit (W/T) and dependent clauses per T-unit (DC/T), both of which were significantly related to the holistic ratings in an analysis of variance. What is also strange is that the measure of the number of coordinating conjunctions was not significantly related to holistic rating but did emerge as a discriminant factor. It is possible to do a hierarchical discriminant analysis where the researcher identifies the order that measures will be considered in the analysis, and perhaps that was done in this case. In any case, the results are somewhat difficult to interpret.

Flahive and Snow (1980), in a discriminant analysis relating developmental measures to three program levels (beginning, intermediate, and advanced), found that words per T-unit (W/T) and clauses per T-unit (C/T) together accounted for 54% of the variance related to program level, with words per T-unit the strongest factor (correlating .67 with program level, as opposed to .29 for C/T). They didn't find that errors per T-unit (E/T) or a complexity index were discriminant factors. These results are consistent with an analysis of variance that related these measures to program levels.

Vann (1979), in a discriminant analysis relating developmental measures to TOEFL scores, found that the number of words per error-free T-unit (W/EFT) combined with the number of error-free T-units per T-unit (EFT/T) accounted for 31% of the variance in TOEFL scores. Words per T-unit (W/T) and dependent clauses per T-unit (DC/T) were not important measures in accounting for variance in TOEFL scores. We don't know how these measures related to one another because she doesn't report correlations between them.

Arthur (1979), in a discriminant analysis relating developmental measures to holistic rankings of an intact class by teachers, found that words per minute (W/M), grammatical errors per word (GrE/W), and spelling errors per word (SpE/W) together accounted for 91% of the variance in rankings. This suggests that teachers are looking at overall fluency (number of words) as well as number of errors (grammatical and spelling errors per word) when ranking compositions.

These examples indicate various ways in which the most promising developmental measures can be compared in future studies, but no studies have done a factor analysis or principal components analysis. In a developmental study, a factor analysis would assess the fit between the developmental measures and the proposed number of factors. A principal components analysis would identify how the measures relate to one another in accounting for the variance in an external proficiency measure, whether they pattern into one or more components. These various types of analysis can aid in identifying the nature of developmental measures, how individual measures pattern into larger factors, and how many factors are related to language use in writing.

THE BEST DEVELOPMENTAL MEASURES TO PURSUE FURTHER

Although certain fluency, accuracy, and complexity measures emerged as the best measures of 'development' and 'error' in the developmental studies that we have examined here, there are gaps in these studies because of the different sets of developmental measures and the variety of proficiency measures that were used as the basis for comparison. This means that other measures that were used in a limited context or not at all may prove in the end to be valuable measures of language development. Based on the measures that did prove to be best, we would like to speculate here on which complete and detailed sets of measures should be investigated in future studies for their potential as measures of language development.

First, there is a set of measures that are based on the T-unit or error-free T-unit as the production measure. These include the measures that we have established as developmentally valid (W/T, W/EFT, C/T, DC/T), the measures of error (EFT/T, E/T), and several new measures related to grammatical and lexical complexity. These are shown in the chart below.

best potential measures based on T and EFT	
fluency	W/T, W/EFT
grammatical complexity	C/T, DC/T, VP/T
lexical complexity	WT/T, LWT/T, SWT/T
accuracy	EFT/T, E/T

For grammatical complexity, we want to maintain a distinction between the four types of finite clauses and the seven types of finite and non-finite verb phrases. When we measure the number of clauses per T-unit (C/T), we want to include only the four types of finite clauses (independent, adverbial, adjectival, and nominal), and when we measure the number of dependent clauses per T-unit (DC/T), we want to include only the three non-independent clause types. So we are proposing an additional verb phrase per T-unit (VP/T) measure that considers all seven types of finite and non-finite verb phrases (finite: independent, adverbial, adjectival, nominal; non-finite: gerundive, infinitival, participial).

For lexical complexity, we want to consider some totally new non-type/token ratio measures that might be able to measure variation and sophistication in the T-unit context. These measures are the number of word types per T-unit (WT/T), the number of lexical word types per T-unit (LWT/T), and the number of sophisticated word types per T-unit (SWT/T). Perhaps these measures will be able to describe variation and sophistication in a way that is independent of length (number of tokens).

There is also a set of measures that are based on the clause or error-free clause as the production measure. These include the measures that we have established as developmentally valid (W/C, DC/C), clause-based measures of error (EFC/C, E/C), and several new measures related to fluency and grammatical and lexical complexity. These are shown in the chart below.

best potential measures based on C and EFC	
fluency	W/C, W/EFC
grammatical complexity	DC/C, VP/C
lexical complexity	WT/C, LWT/C, SWT/C
accuracy	EFC/C, E/C

For fluency, we want to consider the words per error-free clause (W/EFC) measure because of its relationship to the words per error-free T-unit (W/EFT) measure already established. For grammatical complexity, we also want to consider a verb phrase per clauses (VP/C) measure in order to include all seven types of finite and non-finite verb phrases in our consideration of clause complexity. For lexical complexity, we also want to consider the relationship between lexical types and clauses in measures of word types per clause (WT/C), lexical word types per clause (LWT/C), and sophisticated word types per clause (SWT/C).

We think that comparisons between the T-unit-based measures and the clause-based measures should be done to determine which set is the most developmentally and crosslinguistically valid, or whether some combination of measures from both lists is more valid. Ishikawa (1995) demonstrated that the clause context is more useful in measuring early language development, and given Bardovi-Harlig's (1992) arguments against the T-unit, a wholesale shift to the clause as the basic production unit may be in order. Furthermore, for languages that have optional subjects (e.g., Spanish and Chinese), determining T-units is difficult, because the presence of a subject is the primary criteria for deciding whether two coordinated clauses are a single T-unit or belong to separate T-units. Use of the clause may lead to greater crosslinguistic comparability.

Hunt (1965) also showed that certain measures are related mathematically, in that words per T-unit equals the number of words per clause times the number of clauses per T-unit (W/T = W/C x C/T). Accordingly, words per T-unit can increase either through more modification such as complex nominals, or more dependent clauses. Whether or not it is better to measure W/C and C/T independently, or whether W/T can stand alone to represent both should be a matter of future investigation as well. The results from Yau (1991) suggest that they should be measured independently, because W/C correlated with W/T differently at different developmental levels.

Although we have proposed new lexical complexity measures based on the T-unit and clause, we don't want to ignore two other types of lexical complexity ratios that have proved useful. A type/token ratio that calculates the number of word types divided by the square root of two times the number of words (WT/√2W) and a type/type ratio that calculates the number of sophisticated word types divided by the total word types (SWT/WT) can be extended to measures of grammatical complexity, as the following chart shows.

best potential complexity measures based on types and tokens	
lexical complexity	WT/√2W, SWT/WT
grammatical complexity	StrT/√2Str, SStrT/StrT

Because length is an issue in type/token ratios, we prefer the method of calculation used in Arthur (1979), and would like to extend that to a grammatical complexity type/token ratio of structural types to total number of structures (StrT/√2Str). This measure could be used to analyze argument structure types, or verb phrase types, or any other useful structural type. It is also possible to consider a grammatical sophistication type/type ratio of sophisticated structural types to total number of structural types (SStrT/StrT). This would require the identification of an external list of sophisticated structural types, just as the sophisticated word type measure requires the identification of an external list of sophisticated word types. Perhaps the new T-unit-based or clause-based lexical sophistication and variation measures will prove developmentally valid and easier to calculate than these measures, but if type/token or type/type ratios prove to capture something that those measures don't, an extension to measuring variation and sophistication in grammatical complexity may be warranted.

Finally, once a basic set of measures has been established as the most developmentally valid, there are numerous other more detailed measures of grammatical complexity and accuracy that may prove useful in identifying the details of stages in morphosyntactic development. They could be T-unit or clause-based, as the following chart shows.

best potential detailed measures	
grammatical complexity	IndC/T, AdvC/T, NomC/T, AdjC/T, IndC/C, AdvC/C, NomC/C, AdjC/C, InfVP/T, GerVP/T, PartVP/T, InfVP/C, GerVP/C, PartVP/C, DefArt/T, IndefArt/T, Pass/T, CNom/T, DefArt/C, IndefArt/C, Pass/C, CNom/C
accuracy	SynE/T, MorE/T, LexE/T, SynE/C, MorE/C, LexE/C, CorrDefArt/T, CorrIndefArt/T, CorrPass/T, CorrDefArt/C, CorrIndefArt/C, CorrPass/C

The grammatical complexity measures here include an investigation of individual finite clause types (independent, adverbial, nominal, and adjectival clauses), non-finite verb phrase types (infinitives, gerunds, and participles), and other developmentally important structural types (definite articles, indefinite articles, passives, and complex nominals). The accuracy measures here include an investigation of error types (syntactic, morphological, and lexical errors) as well as correct uses of particular structural types (correct definite articles, indefinite articles, and passives). By their very nature, these measures would be more language-specific than the measures we discussed earlier.

We think that these (and other) detailed measures should only be investigated in relation to the well-established developmental measures such as W/T, W/C, or C/T, rather than in relation to some other type of external proficiency measure. They are too detailed to provide an identification of proficiency level by means of one measure, but they can provide information on how stages progress in relation to increases in the more global measures.

THE FUTURE OF DEVELOPMENTAL STUDIES

There are a number of concurrent goals that future research on developmental measures can satisfy. These goals include the determination of which developmental measures are linear or non-linear, which production unit (C or T) is the best for measuring development, how the developmental measures relate to fluency, accuracy, and complexity as factors, how the developmental measures relate to various external measures of proficiency level, how they relate to known developmental stages, and which definitions of 'error-free' or 'sophisticated' are the most valid and reliable.

Once more is known about the best developmental measures, the potential applications include program placement, test validation, end-of-course assessment, trait analysis of holistic ratings, identification of developmental level in research studies, and measuring the global effect of instructional treatments. There is no a priori reason why discrete-point normative tests are better measures for placement purposes than the developmental measures being examined here, and research on the developmental characteristics of existing program levels, the relationship between developmental measures and placement tests, and measures of progress at the end of courses can potentially lead to better placement and promotion decisions. For example, Arnaud (1992) used developmental measures to validate in-house discrete-point grammar and vocabulary tests. And if holistic rating scales are used in placement decisions, developmental measures can also be used to identify the traits in writing that are most salient to those making the judgments, which can aid in training. For example, Homburg (1984) used developmental measures to discover what factors were involved in raters' judgments on a holistic scale used for placement purposes.

For research purposes, developmental measures can provide information on developmental level that allows comparability across studies and target languages. Program levels are not comparable across programs, and standardized test scores exclude the possibility of comparisons when studies don't have them readily available. For example, Chaudron and Parker (1990) used developmental measures to aid in the determination of proficiency groups when no standardized measures were available. Furthermore, program levels and standardized tests do not allow comparisons among learners of different target languages.

The most valid developmental measures can also be used to ascertain whether an instructional treatment being examined for research purposes has any effect on global language development. For example, developmental measures have been used in studies of the effect of program (Carlisle, 1989; Ferris & Politzer, 1981), feedback (Kepner, 1991; Robb, Ross, & Shortreed, 1986), task (Chastain, 1990; Foster & Skehan, 1996; Witte & Davis, 1983), grammar instruction (Frantzen, 1995), planning (Crookes, 1989; Foster & Skehan, 1996; Ortega, 1995), audience (Hirano, 1991), topic (Reid, 1992; Tapia, 1993; Tedick, 1990), and time (Kroll, 1990). Developmental measures can also aid classroom teachers in answering small-scale research questions within the context of their own classrooms.

The goal of this investigation was to determine which developmental measures are the most reliable and valid for analyzing second language development in writing across studies and methods of comparison. The goal of future developmental studies will be to investigate the best of these developmental measures in greater detail, in order to understand the contexts in which they are valid as indicators of 'development' or 'error' relative to the stages that second language learners go through. It will also be important to examine the reliability of the criteria being used by researchers when they apply these measures to the analysis of second language writing. Clearly, the potential uses for developmental measures in pedagogical, testing, and acquisition research make continued research on these measures worthwhile.

REFERENCES

Arnaud, P. J. L. (1992). Objective lexical and grammatical characteristics of L2 written compositions and the validity of separate-component tests. In P. J. L. Arnaud & H. Bejoint (Eds.), *Vocabulary and applied linguistics* (pp. 133–145). London: Macmillan.

Arthur, B. (1979). Short-term changes in EFL composition skills. In C. Yorio, K. Perkins, & J. Schachter (Eds.), *On TESOL '79: The learner in focus* (pp. 330–342). Washington, D. C.: TESOL.

Bachman, L. F. (1990). *Fundamental considerations in language testing*. Oxford: Oxford University Press.

Bardovi-Harlig, K. (1992). A second look at T-unit analysis: Reconsidering the sentence. *TESOL Quarterly, 26*, 390–395.

Bardovi-Harlig, K., & Bofman, T. (1989). Attainment of syntactic and morphological accuracy by advanced language learners. *Studies in Second Language Acquisition, 11*, 17–34.

Bartholomae, D. (1980). The study of error. *College Composition and Communication, 31*, 253–269.

Bialystok, E. (1982). On the relationship between knowing and using linguistic forms. *Applied Linguistics, 3*, 181–206.

Botel, M., Dawkins, J., & Granowsky, A. (1973). A syntactic complexity formula. In W. H. MacGinitie (Ed.), *Assessment problems in reading* (pp. 77–86). Newark, DE: International Reading Association.

Brumfit, C. (1984). *Communicative methodology in language teaching: The roles of fluency and accuracy*. Cambridge University Press.

Carlisle, R. S. (1989). The writing of anglo and hispanic elementary school students in bilingual, submersion, and regular programs. *Studies in Second Language Acquisition, 11*, 257–280.

Carlisle, R., & McKenna, E. (1991). Placement of ESL/EFL undergraduate writers in college-level writing programs. In L. Hamp-Lyons (Ed.), *Assessing second language writing in academic contexts* (pp. 197–211). Norwood, NJ: Ablex Publishing Corporation.

Carroll, J. B. (1967). On sampling from a lognormal model of word-frequency distribution. In H. Kucera & W. N. Francis (Eds.), *Computational analysis of present-day American English* (pp. 406–424). Providence, RI: Brown University.

Casanave, C. P. (1994). Language development in students' journals. *Journal of Second Language Writing, 3*, 179–201.

Chastain, K. (1990). Characteristics of graded and ungraded compositions. *Modern Language Journal, 74*, 10–14.

Chaudron, C., & Parker, K. (1990). Discourse markedness and structural markedness: The acquisition of English noun phrases. *Studies in Second Language Acquisition, 12*, 43–64.

Cohen, J. D., Dunbar, K., & McClelland, J. L. (1990). On the control of automatic processes: A parallel distributed processing account of the Stroop effect. *Psychological Review, 97*, 332–361.

Cooper, T. C. (1976). Measuring written syntactic patterns of second language learners of German. *The Journal of Educational Research, 69*, 176–183.

Crookes, G. (1989). Planning and interlanguage variation. *Studies in Second Language Acquisition, 11*, 367–383.

Crookes, G. (1990). The utterance, and other basic units for second language discourse analysis. *Applied Linguistics, 11*, 183–199.

Cumming, A. 1989. Writing expertise and second language proficiency. *Language Learning, 39*, 81–141.

Cumming, A., & Mellow, D. (1996). An investigation into the validity of written indicators of second language proficiency. In A. Cumming & R. Berwick (Eds.), *Validation in language testing* (pp. 72–93). Clevedon, England: Multilingual Matters.

Dechert, H. W., & Lennon, P. (1989). Collocational blends of advanced second language learners: A preliminary analysis. In W. Odelsky (Ed.), *Constrastive pragmatics* (pp. 131–168). Amsterdam: John Benjamins.

Ellis, N. C. (1996). Sequencing in SLA: Phonological memory, chunking, and points of order. *Studies in Second Language Acquisition, 18*, 91–126.

Endicott, A. L. (1973). A proposed scale for syntactic complexity. *Research in the Teaching of English, 7*, 5–13.

Engber, C.A. (1995). The relationship of lexical proficiency to the quality of ESL compositions. *Journal of Second Language Writing, 4*, 139–156.

Evola, J., Mamer, E., & B. Lentz. (1980). Discrete point versus global scoring for cohesive devices. In J. W. Oller & K. Perkins (Eds.), *Research in language testing* (pp. 177–181). Rowley, ,MA: Newbury House.

Ferris, M. R., & Politzer, R. L. (1981). Effects of early and delayed second language acquisition: English composition skills of Spanish-speaking junior high school students. *TESOL Quarterly, 15*, 263–274.

Fischer, R. A. (1984). Testing written communicative competence in French. *Modern Language Journal, 68*, 13–20.

Fillmore, C. J. (1979). On fluency. In C. Fillmore, D. Kempler, & W. S.-Y. Wang (Eds.), *Individual differences in language ability and language behavior* (pp. 85–101). New York: Academic Press.

Flahive, D. E., & Snow, B. G. (1980). Measures of syntactic complexity in evaluating ESL compositions. In J. W. Oller & K. Perkins (Eds.), *Research in language testing* (pp. 171–176). Rowley, MA: Newbury House.

Foster, P., & Skehan, P. (1996). The influence of planning and task type on second language performance. *Studies in Second Language Acquisition, 18*, 299–323.

Fouly, K. A., Bachman, L. F., & Cziko, G. A. (1990). The divisibility of language competence: A confirmatory approach. *Language Learning, 40*, 1–21.

Frantzen, D. (1995). The effects of grammar supplementation on written accuracy in an intermediate Spanish content course. *Modern Language Journal, 79*, 329–355.

Gaies, S. J. (1976). *Sentence-combining: A technique for assessing proficiency in a second language*. Paper presented at the Conference on Perspectives on Language, University of Louisville, Louisville, KT, May 6–8.

Gaies, S. (1980). T-unit analysis in second language research: Applications, problems and limitations. *TESOL Quarterly, 14*, 53–60.

Gipps, C., & Ewen, E. (1974). Scoring written work in English as a second language. *Educational Research, 16*, 121–125.

Griffiths, R. (1991). Pausological research in an L2 context: A rationale, and review of selected studies. *Applied Linguistics, 12*, 345–364.

Hamp-Lyons, L. (1991). Scoring procedures for ESL contexts. In L. Hamp-Lyons (Ed.), *Assessing second language writing in academic contexts* (pp. 241–276). Norwood, NJ: Ablex Publishing Corporation.

Harley, B., & King, M. L. (1989). Verb lexis in the written compositions of young L2 learners. *Studies in Second Language Acquisition, 11*, 415–439.

Henry, K. (1996). Early L2 writing development: A study of autobiographical essays by university-level students of Russian. *Modern Language Journal, 80*, 309–326.

Hess, C. W., Sefton, K. M., & Landry, R. G. (1986). Sample size and type-token ratios for oral language of preschool children. *Journal of Speech and Hearing Research, 29*, 129–134.

Hirano, K. (1991). The effect of audience on the efficacy of objective measures of EFL proficiency in Japanese university students. *Annual Review of English Language Education in Japan, 2*, 21–30.

Ho-Peng, L. (1983). Using T-unit measures to assess writing proficiency of university ESL students. *RELC Journal, 14*, 35–43.

Homburg, T. J. (1984). Holistic evaluation of ESL compositions: Can it be validated objectively? *TESOL Quarterly, 18*, 87–107.

House, J. (1996). Development of pragmatic fluency in English as a foreign language. *Studies in Second Language Acquisition, 18*, 225–252.

Huebner, T. (1983). *A longitudinal analysis of the acquisition of English*. Ann Arbor, MI: Karoma Publishers.

Hunt, K. W. (1965). *Grammatical structures written at three grade levels*. Urbana, IL: The National Council of Teachers of English.

Hunt, K. W. (1970). Recent measures in syntactic development. In M. Lester (Ed.), *Readings in applied transformational grammar* (pp. 187–200). New York: Holt, Rinehart.

Hunt, K. W. (1970). Syntactic maturity in school children and adults. *Monographs of the Society for Research in Child Development, 35*, No. 134.

Hyltenstam, K. (1988). Lexical characteristics of near-native second-language learners of Swedish. *Journal of Multilingual and Multicultural Development, 9*, 67–84.

Hyltenstam, K. (1992). Non-native features of near-native speakers: On the ultimate attainment of childhood L2 learners. In R. J. Harris (Ed.), *Cognitive processing in bilinguals* (pp. 351–368). Amsterdam: Elsevier Science Publishers, B.V.

Ishikawa, S. (1995). Objective measurement of low-proficiency EFL narrative writing. *Journal of Second Language Writing, 4*, 51–70.

Jacobs, H. L., Zinkgraf, S. A., Wormuth, D. R., Harfiel, V. F., & Hughey, J. B. (1981). *Testing ESL composition: A practical approach.* Rowley, MA: Newbury House.

Johnson, K. E. (1992). Cognitive strategies and second language writers: A re-evaluation of sentence combining. *Journal of second language writing, 1*, 61–75.

Kaczmarek, C. M. (1980). Scoring and rating essay tasks. In J. W. Oller & K. Perkins (Eds.), *Research in language testing* (pp. 151–159). Rowley, MA: Newbury House.

Kameen, P. T. (1979). Syntactic skill and ESL writing quality. In C. Yorio, K. Perkins, & J. Schachter (Eds.), *On TESOL '79: The learner in focus* (pp. 343–364). Washington, D. C.: TESOL.

Kawata, K. (1992). Evaluation of free English composition. *CASELE Research Bulletin, 22*, 49–53.

Kepner, C. G. (1991). An experiment in the relationship of types of written feedback to the development of second-language writing skills. *Modern Language Journal, 75*, 305–313.

Kroll, B. (1990). What does time buy? ESL student performance on home versus class compositions. In B. Kroll (Ed.), *Second language writing: Research insights for the classroom* (pp. 140–154). Cambridge, MA: Cambridge University Press.

LaBrant, L. L. (1934). Changing sentence structure of children. *Elementary English Review, 11*, 59–65, 85–86.

Larsen-Freeman, D. (1978). An ESL index of development. *TESOL Quarterly, 12*, 439–448.

Larsen-Freeman, D. (1983). Assessing global second language proficiency. In H. W. Seliger & M. Long (Eds.), *Classroom-oriented research in second language acquisition* (pp. 287–304). Rowley, MA: Newbury House.

Larsen-Freeman, D., & Strom, V. (1977). The construction of a second language acquisition index of development. *Language Learning, 27*, 123–34.

Laufer, B. (1994). The lexical profile of second language writing: Does it change over time? *RELC Journal, 25,* 21–33.

Lennon, P. (1990). Investigating fluency in EFL: A quantitative approach. *Language Learning, 40,* 387–417.

Linnarud, M. (1986). *Lexis in composition: A performance analysis of Swedish learners' written English.* Sweden: Gleerup.

Logan, G. D. (1988). Toward an instance theory of automatization. *Psychological Review, 95,* 492–527.

MacKay, D. G. (1982). The problems of flexibility, fluency, and speed-accuracy tradeoff in skilled behavior. *Psychological Review, 89,* 483–506.

McClure, E. (1991). A comparison of lexical strategies in L1 and L2 written English narratives. *Pragmatics and Language Learning, 2,* 141–154.

McLaughlin, B. (1990). Restructuring. *Applied Linguistics, 11,* 113–128.

Mellon, J. C. (1979). Issues in the theory and practice of sentence combining: A twenty-year perspective. In D. A. Daiker, A. Kerek, & M. Morenberg (Eds.), *Sentence combining and the teaching of writing* (pp. 1–38). Akron, OH: University of Akron.

Mendelsohn, D. J. (1983). The case for considering syntactic maturity in ESL and EFL. International Review of *Applied Linguistics, 21,* 299–311.

Monroe, J. H. (1975). Measuring and enhancing syntactic fluency in French. *The French Review, 48,* 1023–1031.

Nas, G. (1975). *Determining the communicative value of written discourse produced by L2 learners.* Utrecht, The Netherlands: Institute of Applied Linguistics.

Neuman, R. (1977). *An attempt to define through error analysis the intermediate ESL level at UCLA.* Unpublished thesis, University of California at Los Angeles.

Newell, A. (1990). Unified theories of cognition. Cambridge, MA: Harvard University Press.

Newmark, L., & Reibel, D. A. (1968). Necessity in language learning. *International Review of Applied Linguistics in Language Teaching 2,* 145–164.

Nihalani, N. K. (1981). The quest for the L2 index of development. *RELC Journal, 12,* 50–56.

O'Donnell, R. C., Griffin, W. J., & Norris, R. C. (1967). *Syntax of kindergarten and elementary school children: A transformational analysis* (NCTE Research Report No. 8). Champaign, IL.: National Council of Teachers of English.

O'Donnell, R. C. (1976). A critique of some indices of syntactic maturity. *Research in the Teaching of English, 10,* 33–38.

Ortega, L. (1995). *Planning and second language oral performance.* Unpublished MA thesis, University of Hawai'i at Mānoa.

Perkins, K. (1980). Using objective methods of attained writing proficiency to discriminate among holistic evaluations. *TESOL Quarterly, 14,* 61–69.

Perkins, K. (1983). On the use of composition scoring techniques, objective measures, and objective tests to evaluate ESL writing ability. *TESOL Quarterly, 17*, 651–671.

Perkins, K., & Leahy, R. (1980). Using objective measures of composition to compare native and non-native compositions. In R. Silverstein (Ed.), *Occasional Papers in Linguistics, No. 6* (pp. 306–316). Carbondale: Southern Illinois University.

Péry-Woodley, M.-P. (1991). State of the art: Writing in L1 and L2: Analysing and evaluating learners' texts. *Language Teaching, 24*, 69–83.

Pica, T. (1983). Adult acquisition of English as a second language under different conditions of exposure. *Language Learning, 33*, 465–497.

Polio, C. G. (1997). Measures of linguistic accuracy in second language writing research. *Language Learning, 47*, 101–143.

Reid, J. (1992). A computer text analysis of four cohesion devices in English discourse by native and nonnative writers. *Journal of Second Language Writing, 1*, 79–107.

Rifkin, B., & Roberts, F. D. (1995). Error gravity: A critical review of research design. *Language Learning, 45*, 511–537.

Robb, T., Ross, S., & Shortreed, I. (1986). Salience of feedback on error and its effect on EFL writing quality. *TESOL Quarterly, 20*, 83–95.

Schmidt, R. (1990). The role of consciousness in second language learning. *Applied Linguistics, 11*, 129–158.

Schmidt, R. (1992). Psychological mechanisms underlying second language fluency. *Studies in Second Language Acquisition, 14*, 357–385.

Schneider, M., & Connor, U. (1991). Analyzing topical structure in ESL essays: Not all topics are equal. *Studies in Second Language Acquisition, 12*, 411–427.

Scott, M. S., & Tucker, G. R. (1974). Error analysis and English-language strategies of Arab students. *Language Learning, 24*, 69–97.

Servan-Schreiber, E., & Anderson, J. R. (1990). Learning artificial grammars with competitive chunking. Journal of Experimental Psychology: *Learning, Memory, and Cognition, 16*, 592–608.

Sharma, A. (1980). Syntactic maturity: Assessing writing proficiency in a second language. In R. Silverstein (Ed.), *Occasional Papers in Linguistics, No. 6* (pp. 318–325). Carbondale: Southern Illinois University.

Shuqiang, Z. (1987). Cognitive complexity and written production in English as a second language. *Language Learning, 37*, 469–481.

Sweedler-Brown, C. O. (1993). ESL essay evaluation: The influence of sentence-level and rhetorical features. *Journal of Second Language Writing, 2*, 3–17.

Tapia, E. (1993). *Cognitive demand as a factor in interlanguage syntax: A study in topics and texts.* Unpublished Dissertation, Indiana University.

Tedick, D. (1990). ESL writing assessment: Subject-matter knowledge and its impact on performance. *English for Specific Purposes, 9,* 123–43.

Thomas, M. (1994). Assessment of L2 proficiency in second language acquisition research. *Language Learning, 44,* 307–336.

Tomita, Y. (1990). T-unit o mochiita kokosei no jiyu eisaku bun noryoku no sokutei (Assessing the writing ability of high school students with the use of T-units). *Step Bulletin, 2,* 14–28.

Towell, R., Hawkins, R., & Bazergui, N. (1996). The development of fluency in advanced learners of French. *Applied Linguistics, 17,* 84–119.

Ure, J. (1971). Lexical density and register differentiation. In G. E. Perren & J. L. M. Trim (Eds.), *Applications of linguistics.* Cambridge: Cambridge University Press.

Vann, R. J. (1979). Oral and written syntactic relationships in second language learning. In C. Yorio, K. Perkins, & J. Schachter (Eds.), *On TESOL '79: The learner in focus (pp.* 322–329). Washington, D. C.: TESOL.

Vaughan, C. (1991). Holistic assessment: What goes on in the rater's mind? In L. Hamp-Lyons (Ed.), *Assessing second language writing in academic contexts* (pp. 111–125). Norwood, NJ: Ablex Publishing Corporation.

Witte, S. P., & Davis, A. S. (1983). The stability of T-unit length in the written discourse of college freshmen: A second study. *Research in the Teaching of English, 16,* 71–84.

Witte, S. P., & Faigley, L. L. (1981). Coherence, cohesion and writing quality. *College Composition and Communication, 32,* 189–204.

Yau, M. (1991). The role of language factors in second language writing. In L. Malave & G. Duquette (Eds.), *Language, culture and cognition: A collection of studies in first and second language acquisition* (pp. 266–283). Clevedon, England: Multilingual Matters.

Young, R. (1995). Discontinuous interlanguage development and its implications for oral proficiency rating scales. *Applied Language Learning, 6,* 13–26.

Zamel, V. (1995). Strangers in academia: The experiences of faculty and ESL students across the curriculum. *College Composition and Communication, 46,* 506–521.

Zughoul, M. R. (1991). Lexical choice: Towards writing problematic word lists. International Review of *Applied Linguistics, 29,* 45–60.

APPENDIX A: DEVELOPMENTAL MEASURES

FLUENCY MEASURES

type	measure	code	calculation
frequency	words	W	number of words
frequency	verbs	V	number of verbs
frequency	clauses	C	number of clauses
frequency	sentences	S	number of sentences
frequency	T-units	T	number of T-units
frequency	words in T-units	WT	number of words in T-units
frequency	words in clauses	WC	number of words in clauses
frequency	words in error-free T-units	WEFT	number of words in error-free T-units
frequency	words in error-free clauses	WEFC	number of words in error-free clauses
ratio	words per minute	W/M	number of words per minute
ratio	clause length	W/C	number of words per clauses
ratio	sentence length	W/S	number of words per sentences
ratio	T-unit length	W/T	number of words per T-units
ratio	error-free T-unit length	W/EFT	number of words per error-free T-units
ratio	error-free clause length	W/EFC	number of words per error-free clauses
ratio	words in complex nominals per T-unit	WCN/T	number of words in complex nominals per T-units
ratio	words in complex nominals per clause	WCN/C	number of words in complex nominals per clauses

ACCURACY MEASURES

type	measure	code	calculation
frequency	error-free T-units	EFT	number of error-free T-units
frequency	error-free clauses	EFC	number of error-free clauses
frequency	errors	E	number of errors
frequency	first-degree errors	1DE	number of 1st-degree errors (completely understandable)
frequency	second-degree errors	2DE	number of 2nd-degree errors (understandable only from context)
frequency	third-degree errors	3DE	number of 3rd-degree errors (completely interferes with understanding)
frequency	correct connectors	CorrCN	number of connectors used correctly
frequency	correct pronouns	CorrPN	number of pronouns used correctly
frequency	correct articles	CorrART	number of articles used correctly
ratio	error-free T-unit ratio	EFT/T	error-free T-units per T-unit
ratio	error-free T-units per sentence	EFT/S	error-free T-units per sentence
ratio	error-free T-units per word	EFT/W	error-free T-units per word
ratio	error-free sentence ratio	EFS/S	error-free sentences per sentence
ratio	error-free clause ratio	EFC/C	error-free clauses per clause
ratio	error-free clauses per sentence	EFC/S	error-free clauses per sentence
ratio	error-free clauses per T-unit	EFC/T	error-free clauses per T-unit
ratio	words in error-free clauses ratio	WEFC/WC	words in error-free clauses per words in clauses
ratio	errors per T-unit	E/T	errors per T-unit
ratio	first-degree errors per T-unit	1DE/T	first-degree errors per T-unit
ratio	second-degree errors per T-unit	2DE/T	second-degree errors per T-unit
ratio	third-degree errors per T-unit	3DE/T	third-degree errors per T-unit

type	measure	code	calculation
ratio	errors per clause	E/C	errors per clause
ratio	syntactic errors per clause	SynE/C	syntactic errors per clause
ratio	morphological errors per clause	MorE/C	morphological errors per clause
ratio	lexical errors per clause	LexE/C	lexical errors per clause
ratio	verb lexical errors per verb	VLexE/V	verb lexical errors per verb
ratio	lexical errors per lexical word	LexE/LW	lexical errors per lexical word
ratio	errors per word	E/W	errors per word
ratio	grammatical errors per word	GrE/W	grammatical errors per word
ratio	semantic errors per error	SemE/E	semantic errors per error
ratio	correct connectors per word	CorrCN/W	correct connector use per word
ratio	correct pronouns per word	CorrPN/W	correct pronoun use per word
ratio	correct article ratio	CorrART/CX	correct article use per required or supplied context
ratio	correct definite article ratio	CorrDEF/CX	correct definite article use per required or supplied context
ratio	correct indefinite article ratio	CorrINDEF/CX	correct indefinite article use per required or supplied context
ratio	correct plural ratio	CorrPL/CX	correct plural use per required or supplied context

continued...

ACCURACY MEASURES (cont.)

type	measure	code	calculation
index	Intelligibility index (Gipps & Ewen, 1974)	IntellIndex	sum of points for the intelligibility of each T-unit: 0=unintelligible 1=partly intelligible 2=completely intelligible 3=completely accurate
index	Error index (Kaczmarek, 1980)	ErrorIndex	number of error-free words minus number of errors divided by number of error-free words (errors = wrong or missing words)
index	Error formula 1 (Evola et al., 1980)	EF1	number of correct usages minus number of errors divided by number of words (applied to conjunctions and pronouns)
index	Error formula 2 (Evola et al., 1980)	EF2	number of correct usages minus number of errors divided by number of obligatory contexts (applied to articles)
index	Lexical quality index (Arnaud, 1992)	LexQualIndex	number of lexical word types plus number of rare word types minus number of erroneous lexical words (rare = not in 4-year secondary syllabus)
index	Lexical accuracy index (Engber, 1995)	LexAccIndex	number of lexical word types minus number of lexical errors divided by number of lexical words

GRAMMATICAL COMPLEXITY MEASURES

type	measure	code	calculation
frequency	reduced clauses	RedC	number of reduced clauses
frequency	dependent clauses	DepC	number of dependent clauses
frequency	passives	Pass	number of passives
frequency	passive sentences	PassS	number of passive sentences
frequency	adverbial clauses	AdvC	number of adverbial clauses
frequency	adjective clauses	AdjC	number of adjective clauses
frequency	nominal clauses	NomC	number of nominal clauses
frequency	prepositional phrases	PP	number of prepositional phrases
frequency	preposed adjectives	PAdj	number of preposed adjectives
frequency	pronouns	PN	number of pronouns
frequency	articles	ART	number of articles
frequency	connectors	Conn	number of connectors of all types
frequency	transitional connectors	TConn	number of transitional connectors
frequency	subordinating connectors	SConn	number of subordinating connectors
frequency	coordinating connectors	CConn	number of coordinating connectors
ratio	T-unit complexity ratio	C/T	clauses per T-unit
ratio	sentence complexity ratio	C/S	clauses per sentence
ratio	clauses per error-free T-unit	C/EFT	clauses per error-free T-unit
ratio	dependent clause ratio	DC/C	dependent clauses per clause
ratio	dependent clauses per T-unit	DC/T	dependent clauses per T-unit
ratio	adverbial clauses per T-unit	AdvC/T	adverbial clauses per T-unit
ratio	complex T-unit ratio	CT/T	complex T-units (embedded or dependent clauses) per T-unit
ratio	sentence coordination ratio	T/S	T-units per sentence

continued....

GRAMMATICAL COMPLEXITY MEASURES (cont.)

type	measure	code	calculation
ratio	coordinate clauses per T-unit	CC/T	coordinate clauses per T-unit
ratio	coordinate phrases per T-unit	CP/T	coordinate phrases per T-unit
ratio	dependent infinitives per T-unit	DI/T	dependent infinitives per T-unit
ratio	complex nominals per T-unit	CN/T	complex nominals per T-unit
ratio	passives per T-unit	P/T	passives per T-unit
ratio	passives per clause	P/C	passives per clause
ratio	passives per sentence	P/S	passives per sentence
index	coordination index (Bardovi-Harlig, 1992)	Coord Index	number of independent clause coordinations divided by number of combined clauses (clauses minus sentences)
index	complexity formula (Perkins, 1980)	Complex Formula	score of weighted structures divided by number of sentences: 0=simple sentences 1=modifiers & auxiliaries 2=complex structures 3=subject clauses and absolutes
index	complexity index (Flahive & Snow, 1980)	Complex Index	sum of T-unit scores divided by number of T-units T-unit score = score of weighted structures plus number of words in T-unit divided by number of words in T-unit: 1=derivational morphemes & adjectives 2=relatives, passives, embedded clauses, possessives, comparatives 3=adverbial and noun clauses

type	measure	code	calculation
frequency			number of verb types
ratio	word variation–1	WT/W	word types per total words
ratio	word variation–2	WT/√2W	word types per square root of 2 times total words
ratio	verb variation–1	VT/V	verb types per total verbs
ratio	verb sophistication	SVT/V	number of sophisticated verbs per total verbs (SV defined by researcher, e.g., verbs not on 20-verb or 200-verb frequency list)
ratio	lexical variation	LWT/LW	lexical word types per total lexical words
ratio	noun variation	NT/LW	noun types per total lexical words
ratio	verb variation–2	VT/LW	verb types per total lexical words
ratio	adjective variation	AdjT/LW	adjective types per total lexical words
ratio	adverb variation	AdvT/LW	adverb types per total lexical words
ratio	modifier variation	ModT/LW	modifier types per total lexical words (adjectives and adverbs)
ratio	lexical density	LW/W	number of lexical words per total words
ratio	lexical individuality	ILW/LW	number of individual lexical words per total lexical words (e.g., ILW are words not used by anyone else in the corpus)
ratio	lexical sophistication–1	SLW/LW	number of sophisticated lexical words per total lexical words (e.g., SLW are words not on 20 or 200 or 2000-word frequency list, or words on a list of university-level words)
ratio	lexical sophistication–2	SWT/WT	number of sophisticated word types per total word types (e.g., SLW are defined as above)
ratio	lexical basicness	BWT/WT	number of basic lexical word types per total lexical word types (BLW are defined by researcher, e.g., words on 1000 or 2000-word frequency list)

APPENDIX B: CODES AND CALCULATIONS

CODE	CALCULATION
1DE	number of 1st-degree errors (completely understandable)
1DE/T	first-degree errors per T-unit
2DE	number of 2nd-degree errors (understandable only from context)
2DE/T	second-degree errors per T-unit
3DE	number of 3rd-degree errors (completely interferes with understanding)
3DE/T	third-degree errors per T-unit
AdjC	number of adjective clauses
AdjT/LW	adjective types per total lexical words
AdvC	number of adverbial clauses
AdvC/T	adverbial clauses per T-unit
AdvT/LW	adverb types per total lexical words
ART	number of articles
BWT/WT	number of basic lexical word types per total lexical word types (BLW are defined by researcher, e.g., words on 1000- or 2000- word frequency list)
C	number of clauses
CConn	number of coordinating connectors
CC/T	coordinate clauses per T-unit
C/EFT	clauses per error-free T-unit
CN/T	complex nominals per T-unit
ComplexFormula	score of weighted structures divided by number of sentences: 0=simple sentences, 1=modifiers & auxiliaries, 2=complex structures, 3=subject clauses and absolutes
ComplexIndex	sum of T-unit scores divided by number of T-units T-unit score = score of weighted structures plus number of words in T-unit divided by number of words in T-unit: 1=derivational morphemes & adjectives 2=relatives, passives, embedded clauses, possessives, comparatives 3=adverbial and noun clauses

Conn	number of connectors of all types
CoordIndex	number of independent clause coordinations divided by number of combined clauses (clauses minus sentences)
CorrART	number of articles used correctly
CorrART/CX	correct article use per required or supplied context
CorrCN	number of connectors used correctly
CorrCN/W	correct connector use per word
CorrDEF/CX	correct definite article use per required or supplied context
CorrINDEF/CX	correct indefinite article use per required or supplied context
CorrPL/CX	correct plural use per required or supplied context
CorrPN	number of pronouns used correctly
CorrPN/W	correct pronoun use per word
CP/T	coordinate phrases per T-unit
C/S	clauses per sentence
C/T	clauses per T-unit
CT/T	complex T-units (embedded or dependent clauses) per T-
DC/C	dependent clauses per clause
DC/T	dependent clauses per T-unit
DepC	number of dependent clauses
DI/T	dependent infinitives per T-unit
E	number of errors
E/C	errors per clause
EF1	number of correct usages minus number of errors divided by number of words (applied to conjunctions and pronouns)
EF2	number of correct usages minus number of errors divided by number of obligatory contexts (applied to articles)
EFC	number of error-free clauses
EFC/C	error-free clauses per clause
EFC/S	error-free clauses per sentence
EFC/T	error-free clauses per T-unit
EFS/S	error-free sentences per sentence
EFT	number of error-free T-units
EFT/S	error-free T-units per sentence
EFT/T	error-free T-units per T-unit
EFT/W	error-free T-units per word
Error Index	number of error-free words minus number of errors divided by number of error-free words (errors = wrong or missing words)

E/T	errors per T-unit
E/W	errors per word
GrE/W	grammatical errors per word
ILW/LW	number of individual lexical words per total lexical words (e.g., ILW are words not used by anyone else in the corpus)

IntellIndex	sum of points for the intelligibility of each T-unit:
	    0=unintelligible
	    1=partly intelligible,
	    2=completely intelligible
	    3=completely accurate

LexAccIndex	number of lexical word types minus number of lexical errors divided by number of lexical words
LexE/C	lexical errors per clause
LexE/LW	lexical errors per lexical word
LexQualIndex	number of lexical word types plus number of rare word types minus number of erroneous lexical words (rare = not in 4-year secondary syllabus)
LWT/LW	lexical word types per total lexical words
LW/W	number of lexical words per total words
ModT/LW	modifier types per total lexical words (adjectives and adverbs)
MorE/C	morphological errors per clause
NomC	number of nominal clauses
NT/LW	noun types per total lexical words
PAdj	number of preposed adjectives
Pass	number of passives
PassS	number of passive sentences
P/C	passives per clause
PN	number of pronouns
PP	number of prepositional phrases
P/S	passives per sentence
P/T	passives per T-unit
RedC	number of reduced clauses
S	number of sentences
SConn	number of subordinating connectors
SemE/E	semantic errors per error
SLW/LW	number of sophisticated lexical words per total lexical words (e.g., SLW are words not on 20 or 200 or 2000-word frequency list, or words on a list of university-level words)

SVT/V	number of sophisticated verbs per total verbs (SV defined by researcher, e.g., verbs not on 20-verb or 200-verb frequency list)
SWT/WT	number of sophisticated word types per total word types (e.g., SLW are defined as above)
SynE/C	syntactic errors per clause
T	number of T-units
TConn	number of transitional connectors
T/S	T-units per sentence
V	number of verbs
VLexE/V	verb lexical errors per verb
VT	number of verb types
VT/LW	verb types per total lexical words
VT/V	verb types per total verbs
W	number of words
WC	number of words in clauses
W/C	number of words per clauses
WCN/C	number of words in complex nominals per clauses
WCN/T	number of words in complex nominals per T-units
WEFC	number of words in error-free clauses
W/EFC	number of words per error-free clauses
WEFC/WC	words in error-free clauses per words in clauses
WEFT	number of words in error-free T-units
W/EFT	number of words per error-free T-units
W/M	number of words per minute
W/S	number of words per sentences
WT	number of words in T-units
W/T	number of words per T-units
WT/W	word types per total words
WT/√2W	word types per square root of 2 times total words

study	writers	languages	proficiency	samples	measures	statistics
Arnaud, 1992	50 university freshmen	L1: French FL: English	advanced learners, test scores on grammar and vocabulary tests	two one-hour essays, 6–8 weeks apart, on one given topic; 208 and 241 word samples were used for lexical measures	fluency: W, W/T, W/EFT accuracy: EFT/T, GrE/W, Lex.QualIndex	correlations between test scores and measures on both compositions
Arthur, 1979 study 1 (longitudinal)	14 university students	L1: various SL: English	low-intermediate proficiency, intact class	12 timed, in-class essays on various topics over 8 weeks	fluency: W/M, W/T, W/EFT accuracy: EFT/T, GrE/W, SemE/E lexical complexity: WT/$\sqrt{2W}$	t-tests comparing essays from first half and second half of course
Arthur, 1979 study 2	18 university students	L1: various SL: English	low-intermediate proficiency, intact class holistic rank ordering of essays by teachers	essays on one given topic, no reported time limit	fluency: W/M, W/T, W/EFT accuracy: EFT/T, GrE/W, SemE/E lexical complexity: WT/$\sqrt{2W}$	multiple regression discriminant analysis correlating rankings with measures

continued....

study	writers	languages	proficiency	samples	measures	statistics
Bardovi-Harlig, 1992	86 university students	L1: various SL: English	7 program levels: 1. n=8 (lowest) 2. n=7 3. n=11 4. n=8 5. n=14 6. n=8 7. n=30 (highest)	levels 1–6: 35-minute essays on one given topic level 7: 45-minute essays on one of three topics	grammatical complexity: CoordIndex	no statistical test; only group means
Bardovi-Harlig & Bofman, 1989	30 university students	L1: various SL: English	2 groups based on holistic judgment, same test score range: 1. non-pass: n=15, TOEFL=543–5 67, mean=554 2. pass: n=15, TOEFL=547–5 63, mean=555	45-minute essays on one of three given topics	accuracy: E/C, SynE/C, MorE/C, LexE/C grammatical complexity: C/T	ANOVAs comparing groups on accuracy measures; t-test comparing groups on complexity measure
Casanave, 1994	16 university students	L1: Japanese FL: English	selected students from two intact classes over a three-semester period, TOEFL scores between 420–470	journal entries from beginning, first third, and end of period, no time limit	fluency: W/T, W/EFT accuracy: EFT/T grammatical complexity: C/T, CT/T, CoordIndex lexical complexity: LWT/LW	no statistical tests; no group means; only an examination of individual patterns

study	writers	languages	proficiency	samples	measures	statistics
Cooper, 1976	50 university students	L1: English FL: German	4 course levels and NS: 1. German 200, n=10 2. German 300, n=10 3. German 400, n=10 4. German 500, n=10 5. NS writers, n=10	500 words from essays on various topics	fluency: W/C, W/S, W/T grammatical complexity: T/S, C/T, CP/T, CN/T, AdvC/T, DI/T	MANOVA on effect of levels on measures
Cumming & Mellow, 1996	66 university students	L1: French or Japanese SL: English	French group, 2 levels based on placement tests 1. intermed., n=12 2. advanced, n=12 Japanese group, 2 levels based on TOEFL scores 1. intermed., n=21, mean=438.4, 407–470 2. advanced, n=21, mean=512.8, 473–577	French group: letter, summary, & argument essay Japanese group: placement essay on one of four given topics (no reported time limits)	accuracy: CorrART/CX, CorrINDEF/CX, CorrDEF/CX, CorrPL/CX lexical complexity: WT/W	ANOVA on effect of proficiency level on measures for each group separately: Analysis 1: French group Analysis 2: Japanese group
Engber, 1995	66 university students	L1: Various SL: English	intermediate to advanced proficiency levels, writing score based on 6-point holistic scale	35-minute essay on one given topic	accuracy: LexE/LW, LexAccIndex lexical complexity: LW/W, LWT/LW	correlations between holistic score and measures

continued…

study	writers	languages	proficiency	samples	measures	statistics
Evola et al., 1980	94 university students	L1: Farsi, Arabic SL: English	5 program levels: 1. n=4 (lowest) 2. n=28 3. n=27 4. n=17 5. n=18 (highest) holistic ratings of writing samples based on 6-point holistic scale	20-minute essay on an imaginary accident	complexity: Conn, PN, ART accuracy: CorrCN, CorrPN, CorrART, CorrCN/W, CorrPN/W, CorrART/CX EF1-CN, EF1-PN, EF2-ART	Analysis 1: ANOVA on effect of level, (difficulty, and L1) on complexity measures Analysis 2: correlation between holistic rating and accuracy measures
Fischer, 1984	18 first-year university students	L1: English FL: French	two holistic scales, with 6 levels each: 1. communication 2. clarity	written test responses to a communicative situation	accuracy: E/C	Analysis 1: correlation between communication scale and accuracy Analysis 2: same for clarity scale
Flahive & Snow, 1980	300 university students	L1: various SL: English	6 program levels: 1. n=50 (lowest) 2. n=50 3. n=50 4. n=50 5. n=50 6. n=50 (highest) holistic ratings within each level based on 5-point scale	50-minute essay on one of several given topics	fluency: W/T grammatical complexity: C/T, ComplexIndex accuracy: E/T	Analysis 1: discriminant analysis of 3 collapsed groups Analysis 2: correlation between holistic rating and measures for each level

study	writers	languages	proficiency	samples	measures	statistics
Gipps & Ewen, 1974	751 school-age children	L1: Various Asian SL: English	3 groups defined by years of L2 schooling: 1. <1.5 years, n=228 2. 1.5–3.5, n=281 3. 3.5–5.5, n=242	first 100-words from essays on one of 3 given topics	fluency: W/T accuracy: IntellIndex	statistical comparison between groups on measures (no specifics provided)
Harley & King, 1989	91 6th-grade students	L1: English SL: French	2 groups: 1. French immersion students, n=69 2. French NS, n=22	five 15-minute narratives and letters on given topics	fluency: V, VT accuracy: VLexE/V lexical complexity VT/V, SVT/V–1, SVT/V–2	t-tests comparing two groups on measures
Henry, 1996	67 university students	L1: English FL: Russian	4 school levels: 1. 1st sem., n=20 2. 2nd sem., n=19 3. 4th sem., n=19 4. 6th sem., n=9	10-minute essay on the topic "me"	fluency: W, W/T accuracy: EFT/T	ANOVA on effect of level on measures
Hirano, 1991	158 university students	L1: Japanese FL: English	3 levels based on CELT scores: 1. low; mean=40.4, n=40 2. mid; mean=54.4, n=80 3. high; mean=68.4 n=38	30-minute essays on one given topic, divided into 2 groups differing in audience	fluency: W, T, WEFT, W/C, W/T, W/EFT accuracy: EFT, EFT/T grammatical complexity: C/T, DC/C	Analysis 1: correlations between CELT score and measures Analysis 2: ANOVA on effect of level (and audience) on measures

continued...

study	writers	languages	proficiency	samples	measures	statistics
Homburg, 1984	30 university students	L1: various SL: English	3 holistic rating levels (out of 10): 1. level 5, n=10 2. level 6, n=10 3. level 7, n=10	30-minute essays on one of two given topics	fluency: W, T, S, W/S, W/T accuracy: E, 1DE, 2DE, 3DE, EFT, E/T, 1DE/T, 2DE/T, 3DE/T grammatical complexity: DepC, DC/T, T/S, Conn, TConn, SConn, CConn	Analysis 1: ANOVA on effect of rating on measures Analysis 2: discriminant analysis correlating ratings and measures
Ho-Peng, 1983	60 university students	L1: various SL: English	3 program levels: 1. 2 quarters ESL required, n=20 2. 1 quarter ESL required, n=20 3. no ESL required, n=20	task 1: rewriting the 'aluminum' passage task 2: essays on one given topic, no time limit reported	fluency: W/T, W/EFT accuracy: EFT/S	ANOVA on effect of level on measures
Hyltenstam, 1988, 1992	36 second-year high school students	L1: Finnish Spanish SL: Swedish	3 groups: 1. near-native Finnish-Swedish bilinguals, n=12 2. near-native Spanish-Swedish bilinguals, n=12 3. Swedish NS, n=12	summary and response to 20-minute film without time limit	accuracy: E/W lexical complexity: LWT/LW, LW/W, SLW/LW	t-tests comparing each pair of groups on measures

study	writers	languages	proficiency	samples	measures	statistics
Ishikawa, 1995	57 university freshmen	L1: Japanese FL: English	2 groups, intact classes, both beginning level: 1. n=29 2. n=28	two 30-minute descriptions of a picture sequence, 3 months apart	fluency: W, C, S, T, WC, WT, W/C, W/S, W/T, WEFC, WEFT, W/EFC, W/EFT accuracy: EFC, EFT, EFC/C, EFC/S, EFC/T, EFT/S, EFT/T, WEFC/WC grammatical complexity: T/S, C/S, C/T	Analysis 1: matched-pairs t-tests comparing pre- and post-tests on measures by group Analysis 2: correlations between sums of individual z-scores and measures for each essay and group
Kaczmarek, 1980	137 university students	L1: various SL: English	various proficiencies, two holistic scales, with six levels each: 1. overall ability 2. comprehen– sibility	20-minute essay on an imaginary accident	accuracy: Error Index	correlation between holistic ratings on both scales and measure

continued...

study	writers	languages	proficiency	samples	measures	statistics
Kameen, 1979	50 university students	L1: various SL: English	2 levels derived from holistic ratings of writing samples for a program placement test: 1. good=79+, n=25 2. poor=68–71, n=25	30-minute essays on various topics	fluency: C, W, T, S, W/C, W/T, W/S grammatical complexity: Pass, PassS, P/C, P/T, P/S, C/T, DepC, DC/C, AdjC, AdvC, NomC	Wilcoxon signed rank tests comparing good and poor groups on measures (only 18 of his 40 measures are included here)
Kawata, 1992	44 high school juniors	L1: Japanese FL: English	4 levels based on school grades: 1. grade 5 (A), n=1 2. grade 4 (B), n=1 3. grade 3 (C), n=1 4. grade 2 (D), n=1	50-minute essays on one given topic	fluency: W, S, T, W/S, W/T, W/EFT accuracy: EFT, EFT/T grammatical complexity: PassS	ANOVA on effect of grade on measures
Larsen-Freeman, 1978	212 university students	L1: various SL: English	5 program levels: 1. n=37 (lowest) 2. n=39 3. n=45 4. n=56 5. n=35 (highest)	30-minute essays on one given topic	fluency: W, W/T, W/EFT accuracy: EFT	ANOVA on effect of level on measures
Larsen-Freeman, 1983 study 2	109 university students	L1: various SL: English	4 program levels: 1. n=8 (lowest) 2. n=13 3. n=30 4. n=59 (highest)	task 1: rewriting the 'aluminum' passage task 2: essays on one given topic (no reported time limits)	fluency: W, W/T, W/EFT accuracy: EFT/T	ANOVA on effect of level on measures

study	writers	languages	proficiency	samples	measures	statistics
Larsen-Freeman, 1983 study 3 (longitudinal)	23 university students	L1: various SL: English	intact class at level 4 out of 5 levels, 5 being most proficient	5 essays from each student, one every 2 weeks over 10 weeks	fluency: W, W/T, W/EFT accuracy: EFT/T	repeated measures ANOVA on effect of time on measures
Larsen-Freeman & Strom, 1977	48 university students	L1: various SL: English	5 levels based on holistic judgments of writing samples: 1. poor, n=11 2. fair, n=12 3. average, n=6 4. good, n=14 5. excellent, n=5	essays on one given topic, with an unreported time limit	fluency: W/T accuracy: EFT/T	ANOVA on effect of level on measures
Laufer, 1994	48 freshmen university students	L1: Hebrew or Arabic L2: English	advanced proficiency in English, 2 intact classes	Group 1: (n=23) 2 essays 14 weeks apart Group 2: (n=25) 2 essays 28 weeks apart (unreported time limit)	lexical complexity: LWT/LW, BWT/WT-1000, BWT/WT-2000, SWT/WT-1000+, SWT/WT-2000+, SWT/WT-UWL, SWT/WT-other	Analysis 1: t-tests comparing pre- and post-tests for group 1 on measures Analysis 2: same comparison for group 2 on measures

continued...

study	writers	languages	proficiency	samples	measures	statistics
Linnarud, 1986	63 juniors in high school	L1: Swedish FL: English	2 groups: 1. SLS, n=42 2. NS, n=21 holistic ratings of writing samples based on 3-point holistic scale	40-minute description of a sequence of pictures	fluency: W, W/S accuracy: E, E/W lexical complexity: LW/W, LWT/LW, SLW/LW, ILW/LW	Analysis 1: t-tests comparing NS & SLS on measures Analysis 2: correlations between holistic ratings and measures
McClure, 1991	40 elementary and senior high school students	L1: Spanish SL: English	2 language groups: Spanish-English bilinguals 4th grade, n=10 9th grade, n=10 English monolinguals 4th grade, n=10 9th grade, n=10	narrative account of 4-minute silent film shown twice done within 60-minute class	lexical complexity: WT/W, NT/LW, VT/LW, AdjT/LW, AdvT/LW, Mod/LW	ANOVA on effect of language status (and school level) on measures
Monroe, 1975	110 university students	L1: English FL: French	4 course levels and NS (no reported n-sizes): 1. first-year 2. second-year 3. 3rd & 4th years 4. grad students 5. native speakers	rewriting a simplified passage	fluency: W/C, W/S, W/T grammatical complexity: T/S, C/T, RedC	alludes to an ANOVA on effect of level on measures

study	writers	languages	proficiency	samples	measures	statistics
Nihalani, 1981	29 university students	L1: Indian languages FL: English	holistic judgments of writing samples: 1. satisfactory, n=3 2. borderline, n=12 3. unsatisfactory, n=14 (unknown proficiency, probably advanced)	take-home essays	fluency: W, W/T accuracy: EFT/W lexical complexity: LW/W, LWT/LW	ANOVA on effect of level on measures
Perkins, 1980	29 university students	L1: various SL: English	advanced learners based on the Michigan Test, mean=74.92, SD=5.7. holistic ratings of writing samples based on 3-pt. holistic judgments (no reported n-sizes): 1. pass 2. pass- 3. fail	50-minute essays on one of three given topics	fluency: W, S, T, WEFT, W/T accuracy: E, EFT, E/T grammatical complexity: C/T, ComplexIndex, ComplexFormula	ANOVA on effect of holistic ratings on measures
Perkins & Leahy, 1980	30 university students	L1: various SL: English	2 intact essay classes, with graded essays: 1. SLS, n=15, A=5, B=9, C=1 2. NS, n=15, A=3, B=3, C=8, D=1	take-home persuasion essays	fluency: W/EFT accuracy: EFT, E/T grammatical complexity: C/EFT	Analysis 1: t-tests comparing NS & SLS on measures Analysis 2: various tests comparing grades with measures

continued...

study	writers	languages	proficiency	samples	measures	statistics
Scott & Tucker, 1974 (longitudinal)	22 university students	L1: Arabic FL: English	low-intermediate intact class enrolled based on university placement exam	3 written descriptions of pictures (3–4 sentences each), done at beginning of term and 12 weeks later	accuracy: EFT/T, GrE/W	no statistical tests
Sharma, 1980	60 university students	L1: various SL: English	3 program levels based on Michigan Test+essay: 1. low intermediate range=81–85, n=20 2. high intermediate range=91–95, n=20 3. advanced range=96+, n=20	rewriting the 'aluminum' passage	fluency: W/C, W/T, W/EFT accuracy: EFT grammatical complexity: C/T, CC/T, PP, PAdj, AdjC	t-tests comparing low intermediate and advanced groups on measures (discussed for EFT, W/EFT; non-significant results inferred for other measures)
Tapia, 1993	54 university students	L1: various SL: English	two advanced levels out of 7 program levels: 1. exiting level 4 plus new level 5, n=19 2. exiting level 5 plus new level 6, n=35	two essays, hypothetical and experiential, 35-minute time limit for each	fluency: W, W/EFT accuracy: EFC/C, EFS/S, EFT/T grammatical complexity: CoordIndex	MANOVA on the effect of program level (and topic) on measures

study	writers	languages	proficiency	samples	measures	statistics
Tedick, 1990	105 graduate students	L1: various SL: English	three levels based on program placement: 1. beginning, n=43 2. intermediate, n=43 3. advanced, n=19	two essays, general and field-specific, 48-minute time limit for each	fluency: W, T, W/T, W/EFT accuracy: EFT	MANOVA on effect of program level (and topic) on measures
Tomita, 1990	258 high school students	L1: Japanese FL: English	3 school years, 3 levels based on school grades: 1. sophomores: low, n=23; mid, n=45; high, n=23 2. juniors: low n=21 mid, n=43; high, n=21 3. seniors: low, n=21; mid, n=40 high, n=21	3 written descriptions of pictures, 5 minutes each	fluency: T, W/T, W/EFT accuracy: EFT, EFT/T	Analysis 1: for each school year, correlation between grade and measures and ANOVA on effect of grade on measures Analysis 2: ANOVA on effect of school year on measures
Vann, 1979	28 graduate students	L1: Arabic SL: English	TOEFL scores: range=337–570 mean=420 3 levels based on holistic ratings of writing samples: 1. high 2. mid 3. low	20-minute written summary and response to a film	fluency: W/T, W/EFT accuracy: EFT/T grammatical complexity: DC/T	Analysis 1: multiple regression step analysis correlating TOEFL with measures Analysis 2: comparison of low and high holistic groups on measures
Yau, 1991	60 high school students	L1: Chinese FL: English	2 grade levels and NS 1. 9th grade, n=20 2. 13th grade, n=20 3. NS (9th), n=20	40-minute expository essay on one given topic	fluency: W/C, W/T, WCN/C, WCN/T	ANOVA on effect of group on measures

*** Developmental measures that highly correlate with proficiency (r=.65+), or show an overall effect for proficiency (p<.05) together with a significant difference between three or more adjacent proficiency levels (p<.05).

** Developmental measures that moderately correlate with proficiency (r=.45–.64), or show an overall effect for proficiency for two or more proficiency levels (p<.05).

* Developmental measures that weakly correlate with proficiency (r=.25–.44), or show a trend towards an effect for proficiency (p<.10).

X Developmental measures that show no correlation with or effect for proficiency.

study	***	**	*	X
Arnaud, 1992	W/EFT, EFT/T, GrE/W, LexQualInde:		W/T	
Arthur, 1979, study 1 (longitudinal)	W/M, WT/√2W		EFT/T	W/T, W/EFT, SemE/E, GrE/W
Arthur, 1979, study 2	W/M, GrE/W			EFT/T, SemE/E, W/T, W/EFT, WT/√2W
Bardovi-Harlig, 1992			CoordIndex score decreased with proficiency except for level 6 (no statistics)	
Bardovi-Harlig & Bofman, 1989	LexE/C		E/C, MorE/C	C/T, SynE/C
Casanave, 1994			W/T, W/EFT, EFT/T, C/T, CT/T	CoordIndex, LWT/LW
Cooper, 1976	W/T, W/C, W/S, C/T, CN/T		CP/T	T/S, AdvC/T, DI/T
Cumming & Mellow, 1996, analysis 1	CorrART/CX, CorrINDEF/CX			CorrDEF/CX, CorrPL/CX, WT/W

continued...

study	***	**	*	X
Cumming & Mellow, 1996, analysis 2		CorrART/CX, CorrDEF/CX		CorrINDEF/CX, CorrPL/CX, WT/W
Engber, 1995		LWT/LW, LexAccIndex	LexE/LW	LW/W
Evola et al. 1980, analysis 1		Conn, PN, ART		
Evola et al. 1980, analysis 2			CorrCN, CorrPN, CorrART, EF2-ART	CorrCN/W, CorrPN/W, CorrART/CX, EF1-CN, EF1-PN
Fischer, 1984, analysis 1	E/C			
Fischer, 1984, analysis 2	W/T			E/C
Flahive & Snow, 1980, analysis 1	W/T		C/T	E/T, ComplexIndex
Flahive & Snow, 1980, analysis 2				
6 univ. program levels				
5 holistic writing levels				
level 1 (lowest)		E/T, C/T	ComplexIndex	
level 2		E/T, C/T	W/T, ComplexIndex	
level 3		C/T	W/T, E/T	W/T
level 4		W/T, E/T		ComplexIndex
level 5		W/T	E/T, C/T	C/T, ComplexIndex
level 6 (highest)	W/T	E/T, C/T	ComplexIndex	ComplexIndex

study	***	**	*	X
Gipps & Ewen, 1974		W/T, IntellIndex		
Harley & King, 1989		V, VT, VLexE/V, VT/V, SVT/V-1, SVT/V-2		
Henry, 1996		W/T		W, EFT/T
Hirano, 1991, analysis 1		EFT, W/EFT, W/T, EFT/T	W, W/C, C/T, DC/C, WEFT	T
Hirano, 1991, analysis 2	EFT, WEFT, W/EFT, W/T, EFT/T, C/T, DC/C	W, W/C		
Homburg, 1984, analysis 1		W, W/S, W/T, EFT, 2DE, 2DE/T, DepC, DC/T		S, T, T/S, E, 1DE, 3DE, E/T, 1DE/T, 3DE/T, Conn, TConn, SConn, CConn
Homburg, 1984, analysis 2		2DE/T, DepC	W/S, EFT, CConn	
Ho-Peng, 1983, task 1		W/T, W/EFT, EFT/S		
Ho-Peng, 1983, task 2		W/T, W/EFT, EFT/S		
Hyltenstam, 1988, 1992		E/W, SLW/LW		W, LWT/LW, LW/W
Ishikawa, 1995, analysis 1–group 1		T, EFT, EFC, EFC/S, EFC/T, EFC/C, WEFC, W/T, WEFC/WC		W, C, S, WC, WT, C/S, WEFT, W/C, W/S, C/T, W/EFC, W/EFT, EFT/S, EFT/T, T/S

continued…

study	***	**	*	X
Ishikawa, 1995, analysis 1–group 2		EFC/S, C/S		W, C, S, T, C/T, WC, WT, WEFC, WEFT, W/T, W/C, W/S, EFT, EFC, W/EFC, W/EFT, EFT/S, EFT/T, EFC/T, EFC/C, WEFC/WC, T/S
Ishikawa, 1995, analysis 2	W/EFC, EFC, EFC/S			
Kaczmarek, 1980	Error Index (scale 1) Error Index (scale 2)			
Kameen, 1979		W, W/C, W/T, W/S,		
Pass, PassS, P/C, P/S, P/T		C, T, S, DepC, DC/C, C/T, AdjC, AdvC, NomC		
Kawata, 1992	W/EFT, EFT/T	W/T, PassS		W, S, T, W/S, EFT
Larsen-Freeman, 1978		W, W/T, W/EFT, EFT/T		
Larsen-Freeman, 1983, study 2–task 1	W/T	W, W/EFT		EFT/T
Larsen-Freeman, 1983, study 2–task 2		W, W/T, W/EFT		EFT/T
Larsen-Freeman, 1983, study 3 (longitudinal)		W, W/T, W/EFT		EFT/T
Larsen-Freeman & Strom, 1977	EFT/T			W/T

study	***	**	*	X
Laufer, 1994, analysis 1		SWT/WT-UWL, BWT/WT-2000, SWT/WT-2000+	BWT/WT-1000	LWT/LW, SWT/WT-1000+, SWT/WT-other
Laufer, 1994, analysis 2		SWT/WT-UWL, BWT/WT-2000, SWT/WT-2000+		LWT/LW, BWT/WT-1000, SWT/WT-1000+, SWT/WT-other
Linnarud, 1986, analysis 1		W, LWT/LW, SLW/LW	LW/W, ILW/LW	W/S
Linnarud, 1986, analysis 2		W, ILW/LW	E, SLW/LW	W/S, LW/W, LWT/LW
McClure, 1991		WT/W, NT/LW, AdvT/LW, ModT/LW	AdjT/LW	VT/LW
Monroe, 1975	RedC	W/C, W/S, W/T, T/S, C/T		
Nihalani, 1981				W, W/T, EFT/W, LW/W, LWT/LW
Perkins, 1980		WEFT, E, EFT, E/T		W, S, T, W/T, C/T, ComplexIndex, ComplexFormula
Perkins & Leahy, 1980, analysis 1		EFT, E/T		W/EFT, C/EFT
Perkins & Leahy, 1980, analysis 2				EFT, E/T, W/EFT, C/EFT
Scott & Tucker, 1974 (longitudinal)			EFT/T increased over 12 weeks; GrE/W decreased over 12 weeks (no statistics)	

continued…

study	***	**	*	X
Sharma, 1980		EFT, W/EFT		W/C, W/T, C/T, CC/T, PP, PAdj, AdiC
Tapia, 1993				W, W/EFT, EFC/C, EFS/S, EFT/T, CoordIndex
Tedick, 1990		W, W/T, W/EFT, EFT		T
Tomita, 1990, analysis 1				
level 1: sophomores	EFT, EFT/T		T, W/EFT	W/T
level 2: juniors	EFT, EFT/T		T, W/T	W/EFT
level 3: seniors:		W/EFT, EFT, EFT/T	T	W/T
Tomita, 1990, analysis 2		W/T, EFT, EFT/T		T, W/EFT
Vann, 1979, analysis 1		W/EFT, EFT/T		W/T, DC/T
Vann, 1979, analysis 2		W/EFT, EFT/T		W/T, DC/T
Yau, 1991		W/C, W/T, WCN/T, WCN/C		W/T, DC/T

APPENDIX E: SUMMARY OF RESULTS BY PROFICIENCY MEASURE

*** Developmental measures that highly correlate with proficiency (r=.65+), or show an overall effect for proficiency (p<.05) together with a significant difference between three or more adjacent proficiency levels (p<.05).

** Developmental measures that moderately correlate with proficiency (r=.45–.64), or show an overall effect for proficiency for two or more proficiency levels (p<.05).

* Developmental measures that weakly correlate with proficiency (r=.25–.44), or show a trend towards an effect for proficiency (p<.10).

X Developmental measures that show no correlation with or effect for proficiency.

same level, prof. = longitudinal	***	**	*	X
Arthur, 1979, study 1 low intermed. university class, first 6 vs. last 6 timed essays, over 8 weeks		W/M, WT/√2W	EFT/T	W/T, W/EFT, SemE/E, GrE/W
Casanave, 1994 2 intermediate university classes journal entries over 3 semesters			W/T, W/EFT, EFT/T, C/T, CT/T	CoordIndex, LWT/LW
Ishikawa, 1995, analysis 1 group 1: beginning class 2 essays, 3 months apart		T, EFT, EFC, EFC/S, EFC/T, EFC/C, WEFC, W/T, WEFC/WC		W, C, S, WC, WT, WEFT, W/C, W/S, W/EFC, W/EFT, EFT/S, EFT/T, T/S, C/S, C/T

continued...

same level, prof. = longitudinal (cont.)	***	**	*	X
Ishikawa, 1995, analysis 1 group 2: beginning class 2 essays, 3 months apart		EFC/S, C/S		W, C, S, T, WC, WT, WEFC, WEFT, W/T, W/C, W/S, EFT, EFC, W/EFC, W/EFT, EFT/S, EFT/T, EFC/T, EFC/C, WEFC/WC, T/S, C/T
Larsen-Freeman, 1983, study 3 high intermed. university class 5 essays, 2 week intervals		W, W/T, W/EFT		EFT/T
Laufer, 1994, analysis 1 advanced univ. class 2 essays, 14 wks. apart		SWT/WT-UWL BWT/WT-2000 SWT/WT-2000+	BWT/WT-1000	LWT/LW SWT/WT-1000+ SWT/WT-other
Laufer, 1994, analysis 2 advanced univ. class 2 essays, 28 wks. apart		SWT/WT-UWL BWT/WT-2000 SWT/WT-2000+		LWT/LW, BWT/WT-1000 SWT/WT-1000+ SWT/WT-other
Scott & Tucker, 1974, F] low intermediate. university class 2 short picture descriptions, 12 wks. apart			EFT/T increased over 12 weeks; GrE/W decreased over 12 weeks (no statistics)	

	***	**	*	X
same level, prof. = z-score				X
Ishikawa, 1995, analysis 2 two beginning classes sum of 24 z-scores on 2 essays	W/EFC, EFC, EFC/S			
same level, prof. = course grade				X
Kawata, 1992, FL high school juniors A-D overall course grades; 50-min essay	W/EFT, EFT/T	W/T, PassS		W, S, T, W/S, EFT
Perkins & Leahy, 1980, analysis 2 univ. essay class A-B grades on take-home essay				EFT, E/T, W/EFT, C/EFT

continued…

same level, prof. = course grade (cont.)	***	**	*	X
Tomita, 1990, analysis 1 FL low, mid, hi overall grades 3 five-min pict descriptions 3 high school levels:				
sophomores	EFT, EFT/T		T, W/EFT	W/T
juniors	EFT, EFT/T		T, W/T	W/EFT
seniors		W/EFT, EFT, EFT/T	T	W/T

same level, prof. = holistic rating	***	**	*	X
Arthur, 1979, study 2 low int. univ. class holistic rank order essay, no time limit reported		W/M, GrE/W		W/T, W/EFT, EFT/T, SemE/E, WT/√2W
Fischer, 1984, analysis 1 first-year university students; holistic communication scale written response to situation				E/C

continued…

same level, prof. = holistic rating (cont.)	***	**	*	X
Fischer, 1984, analysis 2	E/C			
first-year university students				
holistic clarity scale				
written response to situation				
Flahive & Snow, 1980, analysis 2				
six univ. program levels				
5-point rating scale				
50-min essay				
Level 1 (lowest)		E/T, C/T	ComplexIndex	
Level 2		E/T, C/T	W/T, ComplexIndex	W/T
Level 3		C/T	W/T, E/T	ComplexIndex
Level 4		W/T, E/T		C/T, ComplexIndex
Flahive & Snow, 1980				
Level 5		W/T	E/T, C/T	ComplexIndex
Level 6 (highest)	W/T	E/T, C/T	ComplexIndex	
Linnarud, 1986, analysis 2	E/W	W, ILW/LW	E, SLW/LW	W/S, LW/W, LWT/LW
FL high school juniors				
3-point holistic scale				
40-min pict desc				

	***	**	*	X
same level, prof. = holistic rating (cont.)	***	**	*	X
Nihalani, 1981 FL univ. students 3-point holistic scale take-home essay				W, W/T, EFT/W, LW/W, LWT/LW
Perkins, 1980 adv. univ. program level; 3-pt. holistic scale; 50-min essay		WEFT, E, EFT, E/T		W, S, T, W/T, C/T, ComplexIndex, ComplexFormula
same test score range. prof. = holistic rating	***	**	*	X
Bardovi-Harlig & Bofman, 1989 university students, TOEFL scores 2-point holistic scale 45-min essay		LexE/C	E/C, MorE/C	C/T, SynE/C
different level, prof. = program level	***	**	*	X
Bardovi-Harlig, 1992 7 univ. program levels: 1–6: 35-min essay 7: 45-min essay			CoordIndex score decreased with proficiency except level 6 (no statistics)	X

different level, prof. = program level (cont.)	***	**	*	X
Cumming & Mellow, 1996, analysis 1 2 levels multiple placement factors 3 types of writing assignments		CorrART/CX, CorrINDEF/CX		CorrDEF/CX, CorrPL/CX, WT/W
Evola et al. 1980, analysis 1 5 univ. program levels 20-min essay		Conn, PN, ART		
Flahive & Snow, 1980, analysis 1 3 univ. program levels; 50-min essay	W/T		C/T	E/T, ComplexIndex
Ho-Peng, 1983, task 1 3 univ. program levels; rewriting a simplified passage		W/T, W/EFT, EFT/S		
Ho-Peng, 1983, task 2 3 univ. program levels essay, no time limit reported		W/T, W/EFT, EFT/S		

continued...

different level, prof. = program level (cont.)	***	**	*	X
Larsen-Freeman, 1978 5 univ. program levels 30-min essay		W, W/T, W/EFT, EFT/T		
Larsen-Freeman, 1983, study 2 task 1, 4 univ. program levels rewriting a simplified passage	W/T	W, W/EFT		EFT/T
Larsen-Freeman, 1983, study 2 task 2, 4 univ. program levels essay, no time limit reported		W, W/T, W/EFT		EFT/T
Sharma, 1980 low and adv. univ. program levels rewriting a simplified passage		EFT, W/EFT		W/C, W/T, C/T, CC/T, PP, PAdj, AdjC
Tapia, 1993 two advanced program levels, two 35-minute essays				W, W/EFT, EFC/C, EFS/S, EFT/T, CoordIndex

	***	**	*	T	X
different level, prof. = program level (cont.)					
Tedick, 1990; three program levels; two 48-minute essays			W, W/T, W/EFT, EFT	T	
different level, prof. = test score					
Arnaud, 1992; FL proficiency test scores; 449-word sample from 2 essays		W/EFT, EFT/T, GrE/W, LexQualIndex	W/T		
Cumming & Mellow, 1996, analysis 2; TOEFL scores, placement essay (no reported time limit)		CorrART/CX, CorrDEF/CX		CorrINDEF/CX, CorrPL/CX, WT/W	
Hirano, 1991, analysis 1; univ. CELT test scores; 30-min essay		EFT, W/EFT, W/T, EFT/T	W, W/C, C/T, DC/C, W/EFT	T	
Hirano, 1991, analysis 2; 3 levels based on CELT scores; 30-min essay	EFT, W/EFT, W/T, EFT/T, C/T, DC/C	W, W/C			

continued…

different level, prof. = test score (cont.)			
Vann, 1979, analysis 1 TOEFL scores 20-min response to film	W/EFT, EFT/T		W/T, DC/T

different level, prof. = holistic rating			
Engber, 1995 univ students, 35-min essay 6-point holistic scale	LWT/LW, LexAccIndex	LexE/LW	LW/W
Evola et al. 1980, analysis 2 univ students, 20-min essay 6-point holistic scale		CorrCN, CorrPN	CorrART, CorrART/CX, CorrCN/W, CorrPN/W
Homburg, 1984, analysis 1 3 holistic rating levels 30-min essay	W, W/S, W/T, EFT, 2DE, 2DE/T, DepC, DC/T		S, T, T/S, E, 1DE, 3DE, E/T, 1DE/T, 3DE/T, Conn, TConn, SConn, CConn
Homburg, 1984, analysis 2 3 holistic rating levels 30-min essay	2DE/T, DepC	W/S, EFT, CConn	

different level, prof. = holistic rating (cont.)

Kameen, 1979 univ. students, 30-min essay, 2 levels based on holistic ratings	W, W/C, W/T, W/S, Pass, PassS, P/C, P/S, P/T	C, T, S, DepC, DC/C, C/T, AdjC, AdvC, NomC
Kaczmarek, 1980 univ. students, 20-min essay, two 6-point holistic scales	Error Index (scale 1) Error Index (scale 2)	
Larsen-Freeman & Strom, 1977 univ. students, 5 levels based on ratings, unknown time limit	EFT/T	W/T
Vann, 1979, analysis 2 univ. students, high and low levels based on holistic ratings of 20-min response to film	W/EFT, EFT/T	W/T, DC/T

different school level, prof. = school level	***	**	*	X
Cooper, 1976 FL 4 univ. course levels & NS 500 words from essays		W/T, W/C, W/S, C/T, CP/T CN/T		T/S, AdvC/T, DI/T
Gipps & Ewen, 1974 SL 3 levels of L2 schooling; 100 words from essays		W/T, IntellIndex		
Henry, 1996 4 univ. course levels 10-minute essay		W/T		W, EFT/T
Monroe, 1975 FL 4 univ. course levels & NS rewriting a simplified passage	RedC	W/C, W/S, W/T, T/S, C/T		
Tomita, 1990, analysis 2 FL 3 high school levels 3 five-min pict description		W/T, EFT, EFT/T		T, W/EFT
Yau, 1991 FL 9th and 13th grades & NS 9th 40-min essay		W/C, W/T, WCN/T, WCN/C		

same school level, prof. = SLS vs. NS comparison	***	**	*	X
Harley & King, 1989 SLS/NS 6th graders five 15-minute pieces		V, VT, VLexE/V, VT/V, SVT/V–1, SVT/V–2		
Hyltenstam, 1988, 1992 SLS/NS high school students untimed film response		E/W, SLW/LW		W, LWT/LW, LW/W
Linnarud, 1986, analysis 1 FL SLS/NS high school juniors 40-min pict description		W, LWT/LW, SLW/LW	LW/W, ILW/LW	W/S
McClure, 1991 SLS/NS 4th and 9th graders narrative of 4-min. film written in 60-minute class		WT/W, NT/LW, AdvT/LW, ModT/LW	AdjT/LW	VT/LW
Perkins & Leahy, 1980, analysis 1 SLS/NS univ. essay classes take-home essay		EFT, E/T		W/EFT, C/EFT

APPENDIX F: SUMMARY OF RESULTS BY DEVELOPMENTAL MEASURE

FLUENCY FREQUENCIES

measure	code	***	**	*	X
words	W		10	1	7
verbs	V		1		
clauses	C				3
sentences	S				6
T-units	T		1	3	8
words in T-units	WT				2
words in clauses	WC				2
words in error-free T-units	WEFT	1	1	1	2
words in error-free clauses	WEFC		1		1

FLUENCY RATIOS

measure	code	***	**	*	X
words per minute	W/M		2		
clause length	W/C		5	1	3
sentence length	W/S		5		5
T-unit length	W/T	4	19	5	12
error-free T-unit length	W/EFT	2	13	2	9
error-free clause length	W/EFC	1			2
words in complex nominals per T-unit	WCN/T		1		
words in complex nominals per clause	WCN/C		1		

ACCURACY FREQUENCIES

measure	code	***	**	*	X
error-free T-units	EFT	3	10		3
error-free clauses	EFC	1	1		1
errors	E		1	1	1
first-degree errors	1DE				1
second-degree errors	2DE		1		
third-degree errors	3DE				1
correct connectors	CorrCN			1	
correct pronouns	CorrPN			1	
correct articles	CorrART			1	

ACCURACY RATIOS

measure	code	***	**	*	X
error-free T-unit ratio	EFT/T	4	8	3	8
error-free T-units per sentence	EFT/S		2		2
error-free T-units per word	EFT/W				1
error-free sentence ratio	EFS/S				1
error-free clause ratio	EFC/C		1		2
error-free clauses per sentence	EFC/S	1	2		
error-free clauses per T-unit	EFC/T		1		1
words in error-free clauses ratio	WEFC/WC		1		1
error per T-unit	E/T		6	2	3
first-degree errors per T-unit	1DE/T				1
second-degree errors per T-unit	2DE/T		1	1	
third-degree errors per T-unit	3DE/T				1
errors per clause	E/C	1		1	1
syntactic errors per clause	SynE/C				1
morphological errors per clause	MorE/C			1	
lexical errors per clause	LexE/C		1		
verb lexical errors per verb	VLexE/V		1		

continued...

measure	code	***	**	*	X
lexical errors per lexical word	LexE/LW			1	
errors per word	E/W	1	1		
grammatical errors per word	GrE/W	1	1	1	1
semantic errors per error	SemE/E				2
correct connectors per word	CorrCN/W				1
correct pronouns per word	CorrPN/W				1
correct article ratio	CorrART/CX		2		1
correct definite article ratio	CorrDEF/CX		1		1
correct indef. article ratio	CorrINDEF/CX	1		1	
correct plural ratio	CorrPL/CX				2

ACCURACY INDICES

measure	code	***	**	*	X
intelligibility index	IntellIndex		1		
error index	Error Index	2			
error formula 1	EF1				2
error formula 2	EF2			1	
lexical quality index	LexQualIndex		1		
lexical accuracy index	LexAccIndex		1		

GRAMMATICAL COMPLEXITY FREQUENCIES

measure	code	***	**	*	X
reduced clauses	RedC	1			
dependent clauses	DepC		1	1	1
passives	Pass		1		
passive sentences	PassS		2		
adverbial clauses	AdvC				1
adjective clauses	AdjC				2
nominal clauses	NomC				1
prepositional phrases	PP				1

continued...

GRAMMATICAL COMPLEXITY FREQUENCIES (cont.)

measure	code	***	**	*	X
preposed adjectives	PAdj				1
pronouns	PN		1		
articles	ART		1		
connectors	Conn		1		1
transitional connectors	TConn				1
subordinating connectors	SConn				1
coordinating connectors	CConn			1	1

GRAMMATICAL COMPLEXITY RATIOS

measure	code	***	**	*	X
T-unit complexity ratio	C/T	1	6	4	7
sentence complexity ratio	C/S		1		1
clauses per error-free T-unit	C/EFT				2
dependent clause ratio	DC/C	1		1	1
dependent clauses per T-unit	DC/T		1		2
adverbial clauses per T-unit	AdvC/T				1
complex T-unit ratio	CT/T			1	
sentence coordination ratio	T/S		1		4
coordinate clauses per T-unit	CC/T				1
coordinate phrases per T-unit	CP/T			1	
dependent infinitives per T-unit	DI/T				1
complex nominals per T-unit	CN/T		1		
passives per T-unit	P/T		1		
passives per clause	P/C		1		
passives per sentence	P/S		1		

GRAMMATICAL COMPLEXITY INDICES

measure	code	***	**	*	X
coordination index	CoordIndex			1	2
complexity formula	ComplexFormula				1
complexity index	ComplexIndex			3	5

LEXICAL COMPLEXITY FREQUENCIES

measure	code	***	**	*	X
Verb type	VT		1		

LEXICAL COMPLEXITY RATIOS

measure	code	***	**	*	X
word variation-1	WT/W			1	2
word variation-2	WT/√2W		1		1
verb variation-1	VT/V		1		
verb sophistication	SVT/V		1		
lexical variation	LWT/LW		2		6
noun variation	NT/LW		1		
verb variation-2	VT/LW				1
adjective variation	AdjT/LW			1	
adverb variation	AdvT/LW		1		
modifier variation	ModT/LW		1		
lexical density	LW/W			1	4
lexical individuality	ILW/LW		1	1	
lexical sophistication-1	SLW/LW		1	2	
lexical sophistication-2	SWT/WT		4		2
lexical basicness	BWT/WT		2	1	1

ABOUT THE AUTHORS

Kate Wolfe-Quintero is an associate professor at the University of Hawai'i at Mānoa, where she teaches in the MA program in English as a Second Language and the PhD program in Second Language Acquisition. She is the director of the University of Hawai'i English Language Program, an intensive English program associated with the Department of Second Language Studies. Her principal research interest is in second language grammatical and lexical development.

Hae-Young Kim teaches Korean and linguistics at Duke University. She received her PhD in Second Language Acquisition from the University of Hawai'i at Mānoa in 2000 with her dissertation, *Acquisition of English Nominal Reference by Korean Speakers*. Her current research and teaching interests include bilingualism, discourse grammar, second language development at the morpho-syntactic level, and curriculum and materials design for Korean learners.

Shunji Inagaki is an assistant professor at the Language Center, Osaka Prefecture University. His principle research interest is in second language acquisition of syntax and semantics.

SLTCC
TECHNICAL REPORTS

The Technical Reports of the Second Language Teaching and Curriculum Center
at the University of Hawai'i (SLTCC) report on ongoing curriculum projects,
provide the results of research related to second language learning and teaching,
and also include extensive related bibliographies. SLTCC Technical Reports are available
through University of Hawai'i Press.

RESEARCH METHODS IN INTERLANGUAGE PRAGMATICS

GABRIELE KASPER
MERETE DAHL

This technical report reviews the methods of data collection employed in 39 studies of interlanguage pragmatics, defined narrowly as the investigation of nonnative speakers' comprehension and production of speech acts, and the acquisition of L2-related speech act knowledge. Data collection instruments are distinguished according to the degree to which they constrain informants' responses, and whether they tap speech act perception/comprehension or production. A main focus of discussion is the validity of different types of data, in particular their adequacy to approximate authentic performance of linguistic action. 51 pp.

(SLTCC Technical Report #1) ISBN 0–8248–1419–3 $10.

A FRAMEWORK FOR TESTING CROSS-CULTURAL PRAGMATICS

THOM HUDSON
EMILY DETMER
J. D. BROWN

This technical report presents a framework for developing methods that assess cross-cultural pragmatic ability. Although the framework has been designed for Japanese and American cross-cultural contrasts, it can serve as a generic approach that can be applied to other language contrasts. The focus is on the variables of social distance, relative power, and the degree of imposition within the speech acts of requests, refusals, and apologies. Evaluation of performance is based on recognition of the speech act, amount of speech, forms or formulæ used, directness, formality, and politeness. 51 pp.

(SLTCC Technical Report #2) ISBN 0–8248–1463–0 $10.

PRAGMATICS OF JAPANESE AS NATIVE AND TARGET LANGUAGE

GABRIELE KASPER
(Editor)

This technical report includes three contributions to the study of the pragmatics of Japanese:

- A bibliography on speech act performance, discourse management, and other pragmatic and sociolinguistic features of Japanese;
- A study on introspective methods in examining Japanese learners' performance of refusals;
- A longitudinal investigation of the acquisition of the particle *ne* by nonnative speakers of Japanese.

125 pp.

(SLTCC Technical Report #3) ISBN 0–8248–1462–2 $10.

A BIBLIOGRAPHY OF PEDAGOGY & RESEARCH IN INTERPRETATION & TRANSLATION

ETILVIA ARJONA

This technical report includes four types of bibliographic information on translation and interpretation studies:

- Research efforts across disciplinary boundaries: cognitive psychology, neurolinguistics, psycholinguistics, sociolinguistics, computational linguistics, measurement, aptitude testing, language policy, decision-making, theses, dissertations;
- Training information covering: program design, curriculum studies, instruction, school administration;
- Instruction information detailing: course syllabi, methodology, models, available textbooks;
- Testing information about aptitude, selection, diagnostic tests.

115 pp.

(SLTCC Technical Report #4) ISBN 0–8248–1572–6 $10.

PRAGMATICS OF CHINESE AS NATIVE AND TARGET LANGUAGE

GABRIELE KASPER
(Editor)

This technical report includes six contributions to the study of the pragmatics of Mandarin Chinese:

- A report of an interview study conducted with nonnative speakers of Chinese;
- Five data-based studies on the performance of different speech acts by native speakers of Mandarin: requesting, refusing, complaining, giving bad news, disagreeing, and complimenting.

312 pp.

(SLTCC Technical Report #5) ISBN 0–8248–1733–8 $15.

THE ROLE OF PHONOLOGICAL CODING IN READING *KANJI*

SACHIKO MATSUNAGA

In this technical report the author reports the results of a study that she conducted on phonological coding in reading *kanji* using an eye-movement monitor and draws some pedagogical implications. In addition, she reviews current literature on the different schools of thought regarding instruction in reading *kanji* and its role in the teaching of non-alphabetic written languages like Japanese. 64 pp.

(SLTCC Technical Report #6) ISBN 0–8248–1734–6 $10.

DEVELOPING PROTOTYPIC MEASURES OF CROSS-CULTURAL PRAGMATICS

THOM HUDSON
EMILY DETMER
J. D. BROWN

Although the study of cross-cultural pragmatics has gained importance in applied linguistics, there are no standard forms of assessment that might make research comparable across studies and languages. The present volume describes the process through which six forms of cross-cultural assessment were developed for second language learners of English. The models may be used for second language learners of other languages. The six forms of assessment involve two forms each of indirect discourse completion tests, oral language production, and self assessment. The procedures involve the assessment of requests, apologies, and refusals. 198 pp.

(SLTCC Technical Report #7) ISBN 0–8248–1763–X $15.

VIRTUAL CONNECTIONS: ONLINE ACTIVITIES & PROJECTS FOR NETWORKING LANGUAGE LEARNERS

MARK WARSCHAUER
(Editor)

Computer networking has created dramatic new possibilities for connecting language learners in a single classroom or across the globe. This collection of activities and projects makes use of e-mail, the World Wide Web, computer conferencing, and other forms of computer-mediated communication for the foreign and second language classroom at any level of instruction. Teachers from around the world submitted the activities compiled in this volume — activities that they have used successfully in their own classrooms. 417 pp.

(SLTCC Technical Report #8) ISBN 0–8248–1793–1 $30.

ATTENTION & AWARENESS IN FOREIGN LANGUAGE LEARNING

RICHARD SCHMIDT
(Editor)

Issues related to the role of attention and awareness in learning lie at the heart of many theoretical and practical controversies in the foreign language field. This collection of papers presents research into the learning of Spanish, Japanese, Finnish, Hawaiian, and English as a second language (with additional comments and examples from French, German, and miniature artificial languages) that bear on these crucial questions for foreign language pedagogy. 394 pp.

(SLTCC Technical Report #9) ISBN 0–8248–1794–X $20.

LINGUISTICS AND LANGUAGE TEACHING: PROCEEDINGS OF THE SIXTH JOINT LSH-HATESL CONFERENCE

C. REVES, C. STEELE, C. S. P. WONG
(Editors)

Technical Report #10 contains 18 articles revolving around the following three topics:

- Linguistic issues: These six papers discuss various linguistics issues: ideophones, syllabic nasals, linguistic areas, computation, tonal melody classification, and *wh*-words.
- Sociolinguistics: Sociolinguistic phenomena in Swahili, signing, Hawaiian, and Japanese are discussed in four of the papers.
- Language teaching and learning: These eight papers cover prosodic modification, note taking, planning in oral production, oral testing, language policy, L2 essay organization, access to dative alternation rules, and child noun phrase structure development. 364 pp.

(SLTCC Technical Report #10) ISBN 0–8248–1851–2 $20.

LANGUAGE LEARNING MOTIVATION: PATHWAYS TO THE NEW CENTURY

REBECCA L. OXFORD
(Editor)

This volume chronicles a revolution in our thinking about what makes students want to learn languages and what causes them to persist in that difficult and rewarding adventure. Topics in this book include the internal structures of and external connections with foreign language motivation; exploring adult language learning motivation, self-efficacy, and anxiety; comparing the motivations and learning strategies of students of Japanese and Spanish; and enhancing the theory of language learning motivation from many psychological and social perspectives. 218 pp.

(SLTCC Technical Report #11) ISBN 0–8248–1849–0 $20.

TELECOLLABORATION IN FOREIGN LANGUAGE LEARNING: PROCEEDINGS OF THE HAWAI'I SYMPOSIUM

MARK WARSCHAUER
(Editor)

The Symposium on Local & Global Electronic Networking in Foreign Language Learning & Research, part of the National Foreign Language Resource Center's *1995 Summer Institute on Technology & the Human Factor in Foreign Language Education* included presentations of papers and hands-on workshops conducted by Symposium participants to facilitate the sharing of resources, ideas, and information about all aspects of electronic networking for foreign language teaching and research, including electronic discussion and conferencing, international cultural exchanges, real-time communication and simulations, research and resource retrieval via the Internet, and research using networks. This collection presents a sampling of those presentations. 252 pp.

(SLTCC Technical Report #12) ISBN 0–8248–1867–9 $20.

LANGUAGE LEARNING STRATEGIES AROUND THE WORLD: CROSS-CULTURAL PERSPECTIVES

REBECCA L. OXFORD
(*Editor*)

Language learning strategies are the specific steps students take to improve their progress in learning a second or foreign language. Optimizing learning strategies improves language performance. This ground-breaking book presents new information about cultural influences on the use of language learning strategies. It also shows innovative ways to assess students' strategy use and remarkable techniques for helping students improve their choice of strategies, with the goal of peak language learning. 166 pp.

(SLTCC Technical Report #13) ISBN 0–8248–1910–1 $20.

SIX MEASURES OF JSL PRAGMATICS

SAYOKO OKADA YAMASHITA

This book investigates differences among tests that can be used to measure the cross-cultural pragmatic ability of English speaking learners of Japanese. Building on the work of Hudson, Detmer, and Brown (Technical Reports #2 and #7 in this series), the author modified six test types which she used to gather data from North American learners of Japanese. She found numerous problems with the multiple-choice discourse completion test but reported that the other five tests all proved highly reliable and reasonably valid. Practical issues involved in creating and using such language tests are discussed from a variety of perspectives. 213 pp.

(SLTCC Technical Report #14) ISBN 0–8248–1914–4 $15.

NEW TRENDS & ISSUES IN TEACHING JAPANESE LANGUAGE & CULTURE

HARUKO M. COOK,
KYOKO HIJIRIDA,
& MILDRED TAHARA
(*Editors*)

In recent years, Japanese has become the fourth most commonly taught foreign language at the college level in the United States. As the number of students who study Japanese has increased, the teaching of Japanese as a foreign language has been established as an important academic field of study. This technical report includes nine contributions to the advancement of this field, encompassing the following five important issues:

- Literature and literature teaching
- Technology in language classroom
- Orthography
- Testing
- Grammatical vs. pragmatic approaches to language teaching 164 pp.

(SLTCC Technical Report #15) ISBN 0–8248–2067–3 $20.

THE DEVELOPMENT OF A LEXICAL TONE PHONOLOGY IN AMERICAN ADULT LEARNERS OF STANDARD MANDARIN CHINESE

SYLVIA HENEL SUN

The study reported is based on an assessment of three decades of research on the SLA of Mandarin tone. It investigates whether differences in learners' tone perception and production are related to differences in the effects of certain linguistic, task, and learner factors. The learners of focus are American students of Mandarin in Beijing, China. Their performances on two perception and three production tasks are analyzed through a host of variables and methods of quantification.

(SLTCC Technical Report #16) ISBN 0–8248–2068–1 $20.

SECOND LANGUAGE DEVELOPMENT IN WRITING: MEASURES OF FLUENCY, ACCURACY, AND COMPLEXITY

KATE WOLFE-QUINTERO, SHUNJI INAGAKI, & HAE-YOUNG KIM

In this book, the authors analyze and compare the ways that fluency, accuracy, grammatical complexity, and lexical complexity have been measured in studies of language development in second language writing. More than 100 developmental measures are examined, with detailed comparisons of the results across the studies that have used each measure. The authors discuss the theoretical foundations for each type of developmental measure, and they consider the relationship between developmental measures and various types of proficiency measures. They also examine criteria for determining which developmental measures are the most successful, and they suggest which measures are the most promising for continuing work on language development.

(SLTCC Technical Report #17) ISBN 0–8248–2069–X $20.

DESIGNING SECOND LANGUAGE PERFORMANCE ASSESSMENTS

JOHN M. NORRIS, JAMES DEAN BROWN, THOM HUDSON, & JIM YOSHIOKA

This technical report focuses on the decision-making potential provided by second language performance assessments. The authors first situate performance assessment within a broader discussion of alternatives in language assessment and in educational assessment in general. They then discuss issues in performance assessment design, implementation, reliability, and validity. Finally, they present a prototype framework for second language performance assessment based on the integration of theoretical underpinnings and research findings from the task-based language teaching literature, the language testing literature, and the educational measurement literature. The authors outline test and item specifications, and they present numerous examples of prototypical language tasks. They also propose a research agenda focusing on the operationalization of second language performance assessments.

(SLTCC Technical Report #18) ISBN 0–8248–2109–2 $20.